Scrappy Project Management®

The 12 Predictable and Avoidable Pitfalls Every Project Faces

By Kimberly Wiefling

A Happy About® series
20660 Stevens Creek Blvd., Suite 210,
Cupertino, CA 95014

Copyright © 2007, 08, 11 by Scrappy About™

First Printing: September 2007
Second Printing: January 2008
Third Printing: September 2011
Paperback ISBN: 1600052053 (978-1-60005-205-7)
Place of Publication: Silicon Valley, California, USA
Paperback Library of Congress Number: 2007935615
eBook ISBN: 1600050522 (978-1-60005-052-7)

Trademarks

Warning and Disclaimer

AUTHOR'S NOTE

"Political correctness is the doctrine holding that it is entirely possible to pick up a turd by the clean end." – Anonymous

SCRAPPY PROJECT MANAGEMENT® contains guidelines that you and your team can use to your advantage to deliver results when the odds are against you. Whether you are a project manager who is new to the field, a seasoned project manager in the midst of a project gone haywire, or a participant in a project where no one appears to be holding the reins, SCRAPPY PROJECT MANAGEMENT will prime your neural pump with ideas that can get you unstuck, moving, and then steering in the direction of your goals.

Like all challenging projects, writing this book was peppered with its fair share of brushes with disaster. For a nearly true look at the hair-raising final moments in the making of SCRAPPY PROJECT MANAGEMENT, see our video at:

http://www.youtube.com/watch?v=KDCJBu3rdvk

Congratulations on picking up this SCRAPPY PROJECT MANAGEMENT guide, and welcome to our scrappy world!

- Kimberly

Meet the Scrappy Guides™

The Scrappy Guides™ is a series of books to help you accomplish the impossible. Those of you who say it can't be done should stay out of the way of those of us doing it!

Scrappy means ATTITUDE.

Scrappy means not relying on a title to be a leader.

Scrappy means being willing to take risks and put yourself out there.

Scrappy means doing the right thing, even when you don't feel like it.

Scrappy means having the steely resolve of a street fighter.

Scrappy means sticking to your guns even if you're shaking in your boots.

Scrappy means being committed beyond reason to making a difference.

Scrappy means caring about something more than you care about being comfortable, socially acceptable, or politically correct.

Scrappy means being absolutely, totally committed to extraordinary results.

Scrappy means EDGY!. . . and is your edge in achieving outrageous results even when they seem impossible.

The Scrappy Guides™ help you muster the courage and commitment to pursue your goals—even when there is no evidence that you can succeed. They are your shield against the naysayers who will try to undermine you, and they will give you comfort during the inevitable failures that accompany most worthy pursuits. When you fail, fail fast, fail forward, in the direction of your goals, lurching fitfully if you must. Sometimes success is built on the foundation of a very tall junk pile.

Let's get scrappy!

BECOME A SCRAPPY GUIDES AUTHOR

Have a "Scrappy" streak in you? Want to write about it? Contact me and let's talk! Email me at kimberly@wiefling.com.

ENDORSEMENTS

"At last, someone has come along who rejects the bland world of 'blah blah blah' project management books that live in the academic ether. Scrappy Project Management has given us the REAL 'dungeons and dragons' equivalent of achieving a SUCCESSFUL project despite the odds and oddities of company culture. Kimberly Wiefling tells you how to fight for what's right and stop being spineless without getting the worst of it. Put this spine on your bookshelf, or in your survival kit. This is THE resource for the power starved PMs who need to learn how to street fight for resources, deal with customer insanity, and dodge the falling rocks as you stay on top of everything. A fighting spirit and a confident strategy is the RETURN ON THIS INVESTMENT."

Michele Jackman, Michele Jackman Enterprises and Adventures, co-author of Star Teams, Players.

"You can take the long, hard road to your dreams, or you can accelerate your success by grabbing a copy of Kimberly Wiefling's Scrappy Project Management and following the rock-solid advice there to achieving results. If you want to build energy, velocity, and momentum toward an outrageous goal, Kimberly's Scrappy Project Management is just what you've been waiting for to help you get those results with more pleasant surprises and fewer disappointing shocks along the way. Some of my favorite nuggets of wisdom from Kimberly's tome are:

- *The top reasons that teams fail are completely avoidable, and due to leadership in absentia. Wake up before it's too late!*
- *How to avoid the rip-tide model of teamwork, where everyone jumps in and drowns together.*
- *Ignore the voice of the customer at your own peril. They are the ones with the money, after all!*
- *Are you a wage slave? If you want to be a great project leader you'd better be able to put your job on the line.*
- *Stop pretending that everything is top priority. Sometimes you've got to choose between your heart, lungs, and kidneys!*

Whether you're on the hook to deliver results for your company or you're getting your business off the ground, you'll learn a lot and avoid some common pitfalls by reading this book."

Christine Comaford-Lynch, CEO of Mighty Ventures, author of Rules for Renegades

"The power of Scrappy Project Management stems from the vibrant, fascinating, and shocking (to some) picture it paints of what is required of the project manager to be truly successful in our incredibly messy project world. The title, the stories, and the no holds barred language Kimberly uses bring to life a unique and powerful view of the PM role—one I think holds important insights for new and experienced PMs alike.

The Scrappy Project Manager may be a shocking persona to those who have been taught that good project management is about the techniques—scope statements, schedules, change control, status reports—rather than about active, highly-involved project leadership laced with huge dosages of personal drive and courage. For those readers, this book makes real what the ephemeral "leadership" term really means on the ground, brings to life what MUST be added to the typical project manager job description for a PM to have a chance on any challenging project, and hammers home the key ingredients for being the kind of project manager that can consistently "deliver the goods" for the business. (What else matters, after all?)

Other project managers have likely sensed and even acted on the need for more than just mastery of specific PM techniques, but felt limited by the culture or manager or process and unsure of how to expand their PM role and influence. For those readers, this book should produce a resounding "YES!" of recognition, a fresh dose of moral support for acting beyond any boundaries they've been saddled with, and practical, energy-reviving, scrappy-esque techniques for doing so.

In short, this book unabashedly puts forward a new, unambiguous, non-shrinking, and ultimately empowering view of what we all as project managers should commit to be and do every day in our project roles.
Cinda Voegtli, CEO of Emprend, Inc. and President of ProjectConnections.com

TESTIMONIALS ON KIMBERLY'S WORK

"Kimberly's 'Leading From Any Seat in the Org' class is the single most powerful class I've attended, and the highest rated class I've participated in. Her teachings have fundamentally changed me as a leader, a coach, and a team member."
Lesley Kew, Intuit

"If you have the opportunity to take a workshop with Wiefling in person, don't walk, RUN to sign up at your earliest opportunity. Her classes are Fun, Entertaining, high energy, and you learn some of the most incredible things. Don't miss it. The only downside to her class is that everything else you take thereafter will pale in comparison. One of the finest class experiences I've ever had."
Dan in California

"Kimberly is one of the most enthusiastic and up-beat people I have ever worked with. She is driven by the belief that it is more than her job, it is her obligation, to make those around her successful. She is an exceptionally quick study with a firm grounding in science and engineering. Kimberly. . . easily identifies choke points to progress as well as opportunities for leverage. She is a model of persistence. . ."
R. H., Director of Engineering

"Kimberly took me to the next level in taking on a leadership role. She encouraged me to success."
Sherry Parsons, Executive Administrative Manager, Earthbound Farm

"Kimberly got me out of my comfort zone and encouraged me to pursue my passion for teaching. She eliminated my fears."
Debbie Gross, Chief Administrative Assistant, Cisco

"Kimberly is a whole energy level unto herself. I call it the "Kimberly Factor". Her passion to give, teach and mentor accelerates people, programs and companies."
Bonnie Savage, CEO Assistant, JDSU

"Kimberly is a driving force of positive energy. Because of her, I'm following my passions. She continues to inspire me to follow my dreams and reach for the stars."
Linda McFarland, CEO Assistant, Seagate

Dedication

For Gram and Pap.

Acknowledgements

This book is living proof that "impossible" is just a measure of difficulty, and requires a team to accomplish. Thanks to all of you who have helped make this book a reality. Am I crazy enough to even TRY to mention all of you? OK, I'll give it a shot, but I'm sure to leave someone out, and besides, people naturally tend to over-estimate their contribution to any success. So, please accept my apologies in advance for any minor or egregious omissions. I will also be delivering my copious thanks in person. For now, please consider yourself tremendously appreciated, because you are. I will never forget everything that you have done to make this dream real! May your karmic debt be significantly reduced by the loving support that you have shared with me through the hardest project of my life (so far)!

Big honkin' thanks to my family, who raised me scrappy. My dad, Alvin, taught me to ignore those who cautioned "It can't be done!" and I love you for that, dad! My mom, Shirley, is the smartest and hardest working person I've ever met. Thanks for always being there for me, mummy! My brothers, Derek and Russell Wiefling, are so scrappy that they make me seem normal and well-balanced. I love you, my bros! I'm grateful to the whole extended Wiefling Clan, the scrappiest family on the planet, for their lifelong modeling of ever-more scrappy behavior.

Huge heaping piles of thanks to Douglas McIntyre, the only person I know of who thinks I'm cute when I am trying to be intimidating and bossy, and who always believes in me even when my own confidence wavers. Considerable boatloads of appreciation to William Andrejko, who keeps the Wiefling Consulting office humming, and fully stocked with rubber chickens and pushing the edges of respectability. Gal-pal hugs to Cynthia Meyer McShane and Algelique DiCio Yoseloff, my truly scrappy grade school girlfriends. Thanks for sticking with me all these years!

Boat loads of thanks to my many colleagues from HP, Candescent, ReplayTV, and Groupfire, who were my constant teachers in the school of life. Buckets of gratitude to my scrappy entrepreneurs, my dear friend Brenda Keiner, who makes me laugh like a hyena, Andy Do, Ralph Scott Penza, Richard Sayle, and many others who did me the great favor of including me in their start-up adventures. Roof-raising cheers to my many fantastic colleagues and friends at

ALC Education in Japan, especially my Japanese sister, Yuko Shibata, and her whole family, who adopted me like kin, strange foreign person or not. Also Toru Yoshikawa, Makoto Honjo, Kenchiro Tachi, Kumiko Saito, Ian Cross, Michael Jones, Mitsuyo Sunada, Megumi Taura, Ryoko Suto, Miki Nema, Yayoi Nakanishi, Ikeda-san, Otsu-san, Shiose-san, and the magnificent Mishima-san... and many more . . . ohmygawd, the list of people I love, admire, and appreciate at ALC is ENDLESS!! Oh, for Pete's sake, I knew I would get into trouble by trying to list each one of you fantastic people individually! These "menaces to mediocrity" at ALC surpass even my own level of scrappiness in their commitment to project excellence and their dedicated support of my work with Japanese businesses all around the world.

Hogs and quiches to my editor, DeAnna Burghart, without whom I would never have let this book out in public, and certainly would not have punctuated properly. (DeAnna, you are the first person ever to make it fun to have my mistakes pointed out to me!) Endless gratitude to the Happy About® team, especially Mitchell Levy and Sneha Laxman, for giving me the impression early on that I really could finish this thing. Rounds of applause for Margaret Di Maria, whose graphics are the scrappiest this side of the Pacific! Copious nods of acknowledgement to those many friends who have opened doors for me that have led to unimaginable possibilities, including the doors of my mind, especially Sherry Rehm, Barbara Fittipaldi, Sandra Clark, Susie Miller, Francine Gordon, Jeanne Parrent, Alex Gray, Natasha Skok, Mara Crags, Ed Gaeta, Bob McDonald, Bonnie Savage, Linda McFarland, Sherry Parsons, Debbie Gross, Joann Linden, Jennifer Vessels, Matt Schlegel, Irina Elent, Todd Cass, Antoinette Burkett, Linda Holroyd, Stephanie Oberg, Julian Simmonds, Jeff Richardson .... Ah, now I know why I resisted listing all of your names. I have been richly blessed by so many generous souls. Even though at this moment I find it impossible to name you all, I can feel your spirit. Thank you all most deeply from the bottom of my scrappy heart!

– Kimberly Wiefling

A Message From Happy About®

Thank you for your purchase of this Scrappy About book, a series from Happy About®. It is available online at http://happyabout.info/scrappyabout/project-management.php or at other online and physical bookstores.

- Please contact us for quantity discounts at sales@happyabout.info.
- If you want to be informed by e-mail of upcoming Happy About® books, please e-mail bookupdate@happyabout.info.

Happy About is interested in you if you are an author who would like to submit a non-fiction book proposal or a corporation that would like to have a book written for you. Please contact us by e-mail editorial@happyabout.info or phone (1-408-257-3000).

Other Happy About books available include:

- The Home Run Hitter's Guide to Fundraising: http://happyabout.info/homerun-fundraising.php
- Overcoming Inventoritis: http://happyabout.info/overcoming-inventoritis.php
- I'm On LinkedIn—Now What???: http://happyabout.info/linkedinhelp.php
- Tales From the Networking Community: http://www.happyabout.info/networking-community.php
- Happy About Online Networking: http://happyabout.info/onlinenetworking.php
- Confessions of a Resilient Entrepreneur: http://happyabout.info/confessions-entrepreneur.php
- Memoirs of the Money Lady: http://happyabout.info/memoirs-money-lady.php
- 30-Day Bootcamp: Your Ultimate Life Makeover: http://www.happyabout.info/30daybootcamp/life-makeover.php
- The Business Rule Revolution: http://happyabout.info/business-rule-revolution.php
- Happy About Global Software Test Automation: http://www.happyabout.info/globalswtestautomation.php
- Happy About Joint Venturing: http://happyabout.info/jointventuring.php
- Happy About Tax Relief: The OIC Solution: http://happyabout.info/oic.php
- Happy About People-to-People Lending With Prosper.com: http://happyabout.info/prosper/

C o n t e n t s

Graphics

Preface

There are plenty of books that attempt to explain how to be a successful project manager. The Project Management Institute (PMI) has created an entire "Body of Knowledge" — the PMBOK — that codifies a neat, clean, surgical description of how a project should be managed from start to finish. It's a nice concept, and in an ideal world these strategies might actually work. In our world, the project leader may not even be involved in the project kick-off, less-than-ready-to-ship products are launched prematurely, and projects run a torturous route that barely resembles the neat, tidy, well-defined process described in the PMBOK.

Real projects are messy! The PMBOK is the #1 best selling project management book on Amazon. That's like having the dictionary being the #1 best selling book in English literature! Scrappy Project Managers know that the PMBOK is a sanitized version of what happens in the real world. It's only the beginning of what it takes to get the job done. My first project management instructor told me, "Get complete, accurate, and validated requirements at the start of the project." This is excellent in theory, and I'd love to work on a project where we have this luxury. Mind you, people in hell want ice water too. That's not happening either. It's just wishful thinking, and that just doesn't cut it in many of the hurricane-like project climates out there. In fact, there are now entire methodologies that specifically recommend not waiting until requirements are complete before implementing them.

Many projects start in the deep recesses of some corporate hallway, or over a beer in some dank little pub. Sometimes the project manager only hears about the project long after it is well under way. Even when a project is carefully planned and formally kicked off, the plan usually changes before the ink is dry on the paper. After that it's victory by successive approximation to an ever-evolving goal. Waterfalls of sequential project tasks have been replaced by cyclones of rapid iteration and massively parallel projects. In the real world, from the time the starting gun is fired, all manner of changes, surprises, and disasters befall a typical project. Teams struggle to keep their footing on the quicksand of rapidly-shifting markets, customer whims, and the vicissitudes of circumstance. Have you ever been on a project where nothing changed? Me neither, so why be surprised when there are changes to requirements, dates, budgets, or staff? Forget the light at the end of the tunnel. It's usually just a break between tunnels. Learn to love the tunnel!

Change is expected. It need not be the surprise guest at your project dinner party. The good news is that most of the obstacles or catastrophes that delay or derail projects are predictable and avoidable. Many project post mortems produce lists of "Lessons Learned" that are identical to the lessons learned in the last project. If we're going to learn the same damn thing every time we might as well call them "Lessons NOT Learned." There's not a whole lot of learning going on when the #1 reason why teams fail to achieve their goals is that they don't have clear goals, and the #2 reason why projects fail is that communication sucks (or, in more politically correct form, is less than sub-optimal)[1].

Behold the Scrappy Project Manager. Scrappy Project Managers don't settle for hysterics and management by crisis, and they certainly don't let something as mundane as so-called reality limit them. They either find a way to seize success from the snapping jaws of defeat, or they invent one. This book is a collection of wisdom on how to get results when the odds are against you, when precedence says it can't be

---

1. Ref: The Bull Survey (1998), The KPMG Canada Survey (1997), The Chaos Report (1995), The OASIG Study (1995).

done, and when the majority of humans believe your project is impossible. It's a book for people who aren't bound by convention, assumptions, or self-limiting beliefs. It's for people who can be counted on to get the job done through hard work, creative thinking, basic common sense, and sheer persistence.

SCRAPPY PROJECT MANAGEMENT is the real deal. It cuts through the BS right to the bone. Structured around the dirty dozen of worst project practices, the 12 predictable and avoidable pitfalls that every project faces, this book describes what REALLY happens in the project environment, and how to survive and thrive in the maelstrom. The converse of the dirty dozen are 12 common sense practices for project management that have been proven to enable leaders to steer their teams clear of avoidable disaster and as much as double their chances of project success.

SCRAPPY PROJECT MANAGEMENT is for those who have the stamina to do what needs to be done in their businesses, and the resolve to go the distance.

The role of project leader is not for the faint of heart. As in many worthy causes, tact and diplomacy can only get you so far, so be sure to have some spunk and attitude on hand when you run out of road with the gentler approach. Sometimes an outrageous act of bravado and nerves of steel will serve you far better than any fancy-schmancy Microsoft® Project Gantt chart. It is during these defining moments that you'll come to appreciate and benefit from the scrappy approach to leading a project. Let's all chant together the scrappy words of Will Willis: "If you're not living on the edge, you're taking up too much space." Enjoy the ride!

Kick Off

"When you're going through hell, keep going." –
Winston Churchill

Project management is one of the most hair-raising jobs in the world. Enormous responsibility, itty-bitty positional power, and the fast pace of many project environments make managing a project one of the world's longest-running stress fests. Many project leaders have no direct access to people, budget, or other critical resources upon which results hinge, and yet they are pretty much completely responsible for the success or failure of the project. And they sure as heck don't get paid anything close to what they're worth! If the project is a success, the project leader has probably broken enough rules and ticked off enough important people that they may not even be able to benefit from the very success they helped create. If a project is a complete and utter failure, the project leader usually takes the rap, and is at serious risk of slapping their hand against their forehead full force while muttering, "What was I thinking?" In this altered state, they may momentarily regret having worked so hard and taken so many risks for a bunch of ungrateful bastards. Fortunately, I have not allowed this kind of experience to make me jaded or cynical. Like Nietzsche said, what doesn't kill us makes us stronger.

Exceptional project leaders are the most amazing business leaders I've ever met. They take on their leadership responsibility with absolute passion and commitment from start to finish. They work without a net, risking failure and daring the impossible to become the unavoidable. They clearly chalk out what needs to be done, define who is supposed to do what, and hold people accountable for following through on their promises. They steadily track status and progress against seemingly unattainable goals, urging everyone involved to make the leap of faith and commit fully to these results. They offer a helping hand or a word of encouragement to those who stumble along the sometimes-rocky road. When they have to deliver unpopular messages they do it with courage and conviction, even when confronting execs with extremely negative news that's guaranteed to twist their knickers. Those who bear bad tidings are frequently unappreciated for the valuable contribution they are making. No one likes to go to the dentist or see the undertaker heading in their direction. A skilled "specialist" who is handy when the godfather needs someone to disappear may be an unwelcome guest at dinner.

Wage Slavery. If you are absolutely dependent on your paycheck to survive, then do yourself a favor—don't be a project leader! In most of the scrappy high-tech organizations where I've worked, the role of a project leader cannot be successfully filled by anyone who can't put his or her job on the line in pursuit of doing the right thing. Never fear, you'll get your reward in heaven. Meanwhile, if you're going to be a courageous project leader you'd best keep at least three months' salary in the bank and an up-to-date resume on file.

In order to deliver results in the challenging circumstances typical of many business environments, project leaders must be absolutely committed to leading their team to success. Frequently, they must execute this feat without explicit high-level support, sometimes with active resistance, and occasionally in the complete absence of any evidence at all that the project is even possible. All of this calls for courageous leadership in the face of fearsome obstacles. Truly extraordinary project leaders must be able to muster an enthusiastic attitude that buoys the spirits of their team members. The attitude of the project leader sets the tone for everyone else on the project. Discouragement is the devil's sharpest tool. You can't afford to be caught monkeying around with that implement of destruction.

LEARN FROM THE MOVIES: In the movie "School of Rock," actor Jack Black plays a loser rock band wannabe. He pretends to be his roommate and takes a substitute teacher's job for a bunch of 6th graders. Spurned by his musical cronies, he soon realizes that he can form his dream rock band from his enthusiastic students. His passion and vision never waver until the jig is up and he's unmasked as an impersonator. Now this guy didn't have a lot of project management training, but he did have tremendous guile and resourcefulness, dodging the principal, parents, and his roommate (the real substitute teacher), while convincing the students they had a shot at achieving their dream of playing the battle of the bands. He and his unlikely rock stars succeed through sheer determination by staying focused on their vision and fending off failure at every turn. Finally, when even he feels beaten and wants to give up, his team refuses to let him quit. By this time they are so committed to the vision he sparked in them that they refuse to give up and drag his sorry ass out of bed to finish it. How cool is that? I'm sure that every project leader has had moments of exhaustion or despair when they needed their team to inspire them. As leaders we've got to inspire them first so that when we hit a low and need a dose of energy they can give it to us. Personally, I frequently look to my teammates to recharge my energy. We don't have to do this alone!

Being a project leader involves being almost ridiculously committed to doing what it takes to deliver the goods in the face of second-guessing and doubt from executives, peers, and even one's own team members. It requires the kind of resolve that can only come from working on a worthy cause, something we care about more than our own security or comfort, something beyond mere "wage slavery." That's fearless project leadership—or at least courageous project leadership even while scared, since we don't always have the luxury of fearlessness. Sometimes we've just got to get it done while we're freaking out about how impossible it seems. That's "Scrappy Project Management" baby! Make this book one of the tools in your get-it-done toolbox, your guide to the vast unknown, where never the spineless shall tread.

Here's the Scrappy Project Management Checklist that we'll use throughout this book (Graphic 1). Tear it out and keep it with you at all times. Really, I'm serious. Tear this page out of this book and keep it in your back pocket. You'll need it. It's what a Scrappy Project Manager would do! Make a copy to nail up to the wall of your office, too. Tape another copy to the dashboard of your car, and yet another on the lower surface of your favorite toilet seat. Why? Because these common sense principles are the ones most frequently overlooked or short-changed on projects, even by those who ought to know better. Knowing "how," all by itself, has never been enough to change a damn thing. Throngs of smart, experienced people have tumbled down the stairs of failure because they overlooked exactly these basics.

Scrappy Project Management Checklist

- [ ] Be completely & unrepentantly obsessed with the "CUSTOMER".
- [ ] Provide shared, measurable, challenging & achievable GOALS as clear as sunlight.
- [ ] Engage in effective, vociferous & unrelenting COMMUNICATION with all stakeholders.
- [ ] Ensure that ROLES & RESPONSIBILITIES are unmistakably understood and agreed upon by all.
- [ ] Create viable PLANS & SCHEDULES that enjoy the team's hearty commitment.
- [ ] Mitigate big, hairy, abominable RISKS & implement innovative ACCELERATORS.
- [ ] PRIORITIZE ruthlessly, choosing between heart, lungs & kidney if necessary.
- [ ] Anticipate and accommodate necessary & inevitable CHANGE.
- [ ] Challenge ASSUMPTIONS & BELIEFS, especially insidious self-imposed limitations.
- [ ] Manage the EXPECTATIONS of all stakeholders: under-promise & over-deliver.
- [ ] LEARN from experience. Make new and more exciting mistakes each time!
- [ ] ATTITUDE OF GRATITUDE. CELEBRATE project success....and some failures, too!

1 Customer? What Customer?

Be completely & unrepentantly obsessed with the "customer."

"There is only one boss: The Customer. And he can fire everybody in the company from the chairman on down, simply by spending his money somewhere else." – Sam Walton

I haven't quite put my finger on it, but there is something about the human condition that retards our ability to be successful project managers. Maybe it's genetic. When we see someone else fail, it's easy to assume that they're just stupid; but when we fail, it's simply an honest mistake or sheer bad luck. "They" should have seen it coming, but "we" were understandably taken by surprise, an innocent victim of circumstances outside our control.

I think psychologists call it the fundamental attribution error, but to me it's the biggest barrier to avoiding predictable pitfalls in a project. It's relatively easy to see where someone else's project is about to hit the skids or could have avoided the long, slow slide into project hell, yet somehow we are still blissfully unaware as our own projects creep inexorably toward Dante's Inferno.

Consider a couple of well-publicized project failures from the 1970s. The first is from a March 15, 1972 article in the *San Jose Mercury News*.

The Moose is Not Loose. Scientists tracking the migratory behavior of moose asked some engineers to design and build a satellite receiver/transmitter for them. When it was ready, the researchers fitted it into a collar that would fit around a moose's neck. They stealthily crept out of their camouflaged den, tranquilized and tagged the object of their scientific desires, then scurried back to their observation post. They patiently waited and watched, but the blip on the radar screen showed no movement. Moose were known to be highly territorial, but the researchers were still a bit surprised at how very small their territory seemed to be. They finally went to check on their reclusive hoofed mammal, only to find him dead in the very same spot where they first attached the tracking collar.

Cause of death? The transmitter weighed so much that the animal was unable to stand while wearing it. Aghast, the scientists went to the engineers, exclaiming, "You killed our moose!" to which the engineers replied, "What moose?" They were oblivious to the fact that their product was going on a moose's neck. Yes, this really happened.

We had a Whale of a Time. This was a bad week for mammals. An article in the *San Francisco Chronicle* that same week described similar misadventures with a whale that wandered into the San Francisco Bay. With much media hoopla, different—but no less ill-fated—scientists laid their plans to track the whale. This giant oceanic creature, affectionately named Humphrey, was escorted from the Bay and encouraged to resume his sub-oceanic travels. Cameras clicked and reporters vied for position on the dock as a tracking device was affixed to the whale's back. The crowd cheered as Humphrey submerged... and immediately disappeared from the radar screen. The transmitter wasn't waterproof!

The indignant scientists accosted the hapless engineers and proclaimed, "You lost our whale!" to which, of course, the engineers retorted, "What whale?" Sorry to say, I am not making this stuff up!

This kind of incredible "oops" in projects isn't limited to mammals or to the last century. In January 2004, *Der Spiegel* chronicled the mishaps of German and Swiss engineers connecting their respective parts of the new Upper Rhine Bridge, who discovered that one half had been built 54 centimeters lower than the other. (That's over 21 inches for those of you in the three countries that still have not converted to the metric system: Liberia, Myanmar, and the US.) Reconstruction costs were massive.

You see how these things go. The most astonishing things can and do happen. What are we supposed to think about a project team that fails to mention that the product they want their engineers to design is going on a hoofed mammal with a pendulous muzzle and enormous antlers? Or one that fails to mention that the product will be riding the back of a sodden vertebrate, destined to go far below the H_2O? Or a team that didn't bother to specify the height at which their bridge will meet up? Assumption is the mother of all such project management calamities. Assume nothing! We've all heard it: "when you assume you make an 'ass' out of 'u' and 'me'." But it's a slippery slope, and projects are awfully busy, so, gee, I guess I can understand why keeping the end result and the delight of the customer clearly in mind gets shunted to the back burner. Gimme a break. I truly would have loved to hear the excuses offered at these post-mortems.

The obvious question for me is how many project teams are creating products and services in the absence of what's going to delight their customers? Smarter people than me have made these mistakes, so I am highly attuned to keeping the customer's desires top of mind in any project where success matters.

Note these statistics. Let me be the first to admit that I am not a marketing genius. In fact, what I know about marketing could be shoved up an ant's ass and still rattle around like a BB in a boxcar. But consider this: more than 50% of all new products fail to meet their goals because they don't meet the needs of their target customers and because they are released with unacceptable quality issues. Even when the quality is acceptable, between 60% and 90% of all new products fail to meet customer expectations.[2]

Do the math. The world is full of gizmos and gadgets that people don't want, don't need, and certainly don't want to pay for. Buoyed by hopelessly optimistic marketing revenue projections that are achieved less than one time out of 600, they get to market before anyone finds out just how off the mark they are.[3] Clunky user interfaces, products that fail to perform as promised, or annoying bugs in the released product create doubt as to whether the designer ever thought about the end user, ever used the product themselves, or, gawd forbid, had talked with even a single real customer. All too often the response is ... Customer? What customer? Oh, shoot, we were so darn busy that we forgot about the friggin' customer!

Who is your Customer? Every team member has an image of the customer in their head, and typically, that customer looks and acts just like they do. However, this image may in no way resemble a real customer. In actuality, many people working on projects have little or no experience of their customers. Their information is secondhand, gathered by sales, filtered by marketing, and interpreted by the project manager and designers. I once worked with a team of people who'd been designing complicated chemical analysis equipment for decades. Several of the lead designers had never operated the instrument. In as little as an hour or a day they could have easily acquired some real insight into what it was like to use one of their instruments, but it simply wasn't a priority. Needless to say, I required them to learn to use the products when I was leading the project. Maybe I'm kidding myself, but I think they actually enjoyed their work more knowing personally how real people in the real world used their product.

---

2. Aberdeen Group, "Making the Case for Collaborative Product Commerce," July 2001.
3. Hammer and Company, "Accelerating Innovation: New Urgency, New Approaches." 2003

Sometimes the customer of a project is an internal person in the same company, sometimes they are an outside person who buys or uses the product or service. In any case, knowing who will be the ultimate judge of success or failure is critical to defining success. Some people are oblivious to the fact that there is a living, breathing customer out there whose needs and wants should be the driving force in the project. Or they assume that the customer is just like their very own self, and create something they think the customer will be happy with. Save us from these kinds of products! That's how Microsoft Windows® was created.

SCRAPPY TIP: *The first characteristic of a successful project manager is to be completely and unrepentantly obsessed with the customer. Get out of your office, visit delighted and dissatisfied customers, ride on sales calls, call angry customers who have abandoned your products for other solutions, interview your family, friends, and strangers on the street. Shadow real customers throughout a day or a week. Swim in the customer's fishbowl so that you know exactly what their pain is and how your product or service is the painkiller that will surprise and delight them.*

Ignore the Voice of the Customer at Your Peril. Of course, no amount of customer-centric thinking will save a team led by someone who doesn't value customer input. A high-level manager at a Fortune 500 company once declared to me, "Our customers should be required to take an intelligence test prior to purchasing the product." While some customers aren't the sharpest knives in the drawer, I believe that truly customer-focused designers can make any product easy to learn and use. Besides, stupid people have money too!

While the key to delighting customers has always been to under-promise and over-deliver, just asking customers what they want is not enough. Henry Ford said that if he'd listened to customers, Ford Motor Company would have been designing faster horses. Customers rarely have the imagination to ask for things totally outside of their experience, like overnight package delivery or fax machines, until after they are invented. But customers can be terrific sources of information about what causes them headaches, what they worry about, and the seemingly impossible challenges that they face. "What seems impossible, but if it were possible, would transform your business for the better?" Ask that simple paradigm-shifting question and you may find the seeds of a billion dollar business.

There is no substitute for personal experience with the customer. As Steve Blank of the Aberdeen Group says in *Making the Case for Collaborative Product Commerce* (July 2001), "There are no answers inside of this building. Getting project teams out swimming in the customer fishbowl is critical to enabling each person on the team to make decisions in alignment with real customer problems, wants, and needs." Cultural anthropology is studying what it's like to be immersed in the customer's world, and I believe that it's the best way to find out what real customers want and need. Ignoring the voice of the customer significantly raises the odds that your product will be in the huge heap of new products that fail to meet customer expectations.

SCRAPPY TIP: *Most teams don't take the time to include the customer until it is far too late. Too busy to develop a thorough understanding of the very people who will judge their project's success, they stumble onward, mistaking activity for progress. Those that do invest in understanding of their target market gain a significant advantage, more than doubling their chances of creating a result that will surprise and delight their customer. Don't settle for "no time to include the voice of the customer" in your projects!*

---

2 If You Don't Know Where You're Going, Any Road Will Do

Provide shared, measurable, challenging & achievable goals as clear as sunlight.

"When I was young I always wanted to BE somebody when I grew up. I just wish I'd been more specific." – Lily Tomlin

Ignoring the needs of real customers is just the start. When most project teams hear the shot of the starting gun they leap into figuring out how to do it—even before they clearly understand what "it" is. This is the number one reason teams fail to achieve their goals—they don't *have* clear goals. Even when teams honestly believe that they have goals, they are often nebulous and ill-defined. Or even worse, different people have dramatically different ideas of the goal, but are under the illusion that they are singing from the same song sheet.

When goals are fuzzy, the project has no specific and measurable finish line. Notions of what defines "the end" of the project hover in a foggy haze. Naturally, each stakeholder has a different idea of what defines success and in which direction the finish line lies. Sometimes people take to milling around aimlessly, shuffling their feet, maybe picking lint off their sweater or kicking up a few clods of dirt while they wait for clarity to dawn.

The point is that these differences must be made explicit, and purposeful trade-offs made among the various criteria. Ask a group of people to draw a tree and each person will imagine and draw an entirely different tree. Similarly, when the goal of a project is not clearly specified, perception of the goal will vary from person to person, making a truly shared understanding of the goals a remote possibility in the realm of pure chance.

SCRAPPY TIP: *A poem that I learned as a kid pops into my mind when goals are unclear. "Fuzzy Wuzzy was a bear. Fuzzy Wuzzy had no hair. Fuzzy Wuzzy wasn't really fuzzy, then, was he?" Even if you don't like poetry, "Fuzzy Wuzzy" is great for a teddy bear, but not for a project finish line. Insist on goals as clear as sunlight.*

Failure Disguised as Short-term Success. How will your team know if your project is poised for a successful completion? If your product performs as promised, ships on schedule, and meets budget and cost goals, will that be considered a success? Not necessarily. For example, one lovingly handcrafted prototype doesn't make for a product suitable for volume production where lot-to-lot variations can introduce all manner of customization. Just because a software program runs successfully in QA doesn't mean users will be able to figure out how to install it, learn it, and use it without inordinate frustration. Just ask anyone who runs Windows! "Performs as designed" is a slight that we reserve for projects that "worked for a while," at least until the package was opened or the check cleared. Project teams committed to their goals need a well-rounded, complete, and measurable definition of success that drives the decisions, behavior, and choices of every stakeholder. Clearly defining success increases the likelihood of achieving it.

SCRAPPY TIP: *No sensible person would jump into a taxi and yell, "Drive like the wind, as fast as you can!" Clarifying the destination is the first step in taking a trip.*

Doom is the Destiny of the Directionless. In the throes of a product launch, teams are going to do what is required, not necessarily what is desired. Critical measures of success simply can't be left to the discretion of an overworked team. The immediate pressure to deliver can overwhelm the judgment of even the most seasoned professional. Anything that is not an explicit goal is unlikely to be given the attention it deserves.

For example, imagine that you are sitting in the "Go/No-Go" meeting for an urgently needed product launch. Without explicit criteria, decisions will probably be motivated by the expediency of the launch, even in the face of significant concerns. Just a bland statement of goals is inadequate, and the fallback position of many project managers—the triple constraint—is insufficient to assure a sensible decision. What is required is a comprehensive and objective set of criteria to determine whether or not it's appropriate to launch.

"Planning a new product without first defining the criteria for success is the equivalent of trying to steer a large boat by paddling with your hands: you will end up wherever the current takes you. However, when the success criteria are properly defined prior to planning, several companies have experienced reduced development times, outstanding customer experience, and revenue/ROI that exceeded expectations."

- E. Gaeta, Director of Program Management, Extreme Networks

The Rip Tide Model of Project Teamwork. With unclear goals, the speed of mistakes exceeds the speed of progress, and team members start to drift rather than paddle. Imagine yourself floating on a raft in the middle of the Pacific Ocean on a dark, cloud-covered, moonless night. Having no idea of where you were, whether you were moving, or in which direction, why on earth would you bother to paddle? Compare this to being on a speeding bullet train where the path and destination are clearly defined. Even if the track runs out a couple of kilometers down the line, a team that trusts their leader will fly down the tracks at full throttle, knowing that more track will be laid by the time they get there.

Projects gone haywire are like rip tides. One person is pulled under by a strong current, so some hero wades in to save the first. Naturally the would-be hero is also ensnared by the violent tide. Seeing two victims struggling, yet another brave soul tosses themselves into the fray. The news channels inevitably report multiple drowning victims. Instead of one tragic loss of life, a whole heap of people meet a watery death.

I've been on projects like this, with everyone thrashing about, struggling to stay afloat. Rather than dramatic heroics, this situation calls for a cool head. Stop first, think for a nanosecond or two, and then act with the common sense required to break free of the unproductive, adrenaline-fueled struggle. Otherwise, one by one or en masse, each person drowns in an overwhelming tide of tasks and demands. Mistakes mount as they struggle valiantly to do what needs to be done. If only one person had the presence of mind to say, "Hey guys, let's step back and think for a moment about why we're here and what we're doing," the team might be able to escape the watery tomb. Instead, they panic. They work longer hours, and work harder, but they most assuredly don't work smarter. In the grip of the accompanying adrenaline rush so familiar to those of us who work in fast-paced project environments, they put in more and more effort, but get less and less done.

The problems grow bigger and hairier. Fixing mistakes takes up precious time desperately needed for other critical tasks. Even if no one notices yet, the project has already started to unravel. Eventually, a critical deadline is missed or a damaging mistake brings the team and curious on-lookers up short. Only then, and usually too late, does someone finally decide, "Something must be done!" At the root of this huge problem tree lies its cause—unclear goals.

Common Sense is Not Common Practice! If you don't know where you're going, any road will do. "Success" must be precisely defined with laser focus, or you'll end up at an alternate destination. It might have seemed like a good idea at that time, but it can be a lot less satisfying.

A project isn't successful if the entire team is burned out at the end, or if key individuals quit in frustration afterward, or if most customers are dissatisfied with the product. What if your product has unacceptable quality issues or must be recalled three months hence? What if the company's branding is diluted by a quality blemish? Are you successful if you ship something on time and on budget but with an undiscovered safety hazard? Most organizations do not include these types of issues in their success scorecard.

And how about your own personal scorecard as a project leader? In my younger days I focused entirely on results, with little regard for the impact of the process on myself or others. I worked myself into exhaustion, became even more irritable than normal, alienated potential allies, pushed people too hard, and said lots of stupid things that made me wish I had a rewind and erase button on my mouth. On one occasion I got into some quarrels with one of my guys. He was normally easy-going, so I asked him what was wrong. He said he was trying to quit smoking. My retort? "Quit after the project is over!" And when another talented engineer complained that the long hours were wrecking his relationship with his girlfriend I told him he could always find a new girlfriend after the project was finished. Although somewhat funny at the time, I look back on my callousness with a degree of remorse. My own personal scorecard now includes building long-term relationships. After all, in the Silicon Valley the relationships last longer than the companies.

Wave Goodbye to the Triple Constraint. It's all too easy for a product development team to mistakenly assume that meeting formal project requirements defined by the outdated triple constraint of schedule, scope, and cost will result in a successful product launch. Proceeding under this assumption plants the seeds of predictable and preventable failure.

Finishing on time with the required features and at the required cost has never been enough to ensure a successful project. This myopic view results from a tendency to focus excessively on features, leaving other critical aspects of success—such as quality, usability, and profitability—to chance.

What Gets Measured Is What Gets Done. While scorecards can take many forms, the key attributes of a useful scorecard are:

1. A complete list of success criteria.
2. A clear description of each of these criteria.
3. Specific, measurable, and actionable targets for each criterion.
4. The minimum acceptable level for each criterion.
5. A prioritization of at least the top three most important criteria.

Savvy project teams use the kickoff to generate a one-page scorecard or dashboard, such as the one shown in Graphic 2, or other simple visual indicators. This requires collaboration from cross-functional team members and any other stakeholders who have the power to weigh in on whether the team did a great job or not—including buying decision-makers, end users, manufacturing partners, and distribution channels.

This scorecard is updated at each major milestone with a status and estimate of what it's going to take to reach the targets by product launch. Creating such a scorecard is easily facilitated by asking the question, "When this product is wildly and outrageously successful, what will people be saying about this product, this team, and this company?"

Project Success Scorecard

Priority for this Project	Item	Description	Minimum Acceptance Limit	Target	Status (red, yellow, green)	Action Required to Change to Green	Owner
#4	Functionality	Minimum viable features to succeed in the market	Minimum feature set agreed to and defined	All musts and top 5 wants	Green	NA	
#3	Quick to learn	Time from set-up to first sample run	No more than 10 minutes	5 min	Green	NA	
#2	Quality	Meets or exceeds customer expectations and internal goals	NPS > 68 and AFR < 2%	AFR less than 2%	Yellow	Cut features to increase time available for quality testing	Bart
#1	Schedule	Schedule hits market opportunity window	Phase 1 schedule + 2 months	Phase 1 schedule	Red	Parallel development of key features	Krista

Graphic 2: Back-of-the-Napkin Style Project Scorecard Example

A one-page scorecard keeps the detailed definition of success visible to the team throughout the project and better enables the individuals involved to make the many trade-offs that will be required along the way. With large, fast-moving teams in distributed decision-making environments separated by oceans and time zones, keeping the detailed definition of success visible is even more important. But even a co-located team can benefit. Really, how many people do you think read the whole requirements document? Unless you sit there and watch them read it, damn few.

SCRAPPY TIP: *A one-page scorecard of critical success factors is far more accessible than an encyclopedic requirements document. The scorecard can be updated by the team at each checkpoint to keep status and progress vs. the goals highly visible.*

Applying the scorecard process with discipline will dramatically reduce your chances of failure and keep your team focused on what it's really going to take to claim a legitimate victory. Create your scorecard early in the project while everyone is still thinking clearly. It's just too friggin' easy to lower your standards when the drop-dead date is bearing down on your team!

> *"Scorecards enabled our project teams to set clear and prioritized goals that they and the management used to track and measure the project development progress and success through product development, product launch, and market success, while removing the ambiguity from the process."*
>
> *— Debra Worsley Hein, Director, Engr. Program Management, Extreme Networks*

The Thrill of Anticipation. No matter how diligent you are at creating clear goals in your project, there will usually be resistance from the CAVE people (Citizens Against Virtually Everything) as well as from reasonable people, because some of these criteria simply can't be easily measured. Others can't be measured until well after the launch, and a few won't be measurable at all, ever. Fortunately, the measurement is the least of it. The practice of defining the criteria and referring back to it repeatedly during the project—and especially at project completion—provides as much or more value as the actual measurement. Like a person on a diet who watches their calories more closely when they know they will be weighing in every week, the anticipation of measurement can sometimes be more important than the practicality of the measurement or the accuracy of the scale.

"Kimberly's scorecard is an effective tool to always keep the team focused on the overall objectives of the project, and to drive the everyday tasks in line with the objectives."

— Natasha Skok, Tallwood Venture Capital

SCRAPPY TIP: *A simple red/yellow/green assessment of whether each item is on track or not is sufficient to remind everyone involved of the shared goals for big-picture success. "What's it going to take to make this item green?" is a great question for generating mitigation plans to get back on track before it's too late.*

The Primary Cause of Product Failure is Preventable. Lack of goals is a completely avoidable and preventable cause of failure, and one that every Scrappy Project Manager should commit to eradicating. Don't settle for anything less than goals that are as clear as sunlight. Without them, your team could end up like the guy with an arthritic hand who prayed "Please, dear God, make my one hand like the other"—only to end up with two crippled hands.

"It always surprises me how teams jump into projects without clearly-defined objectives. I think it surprises them, when they are asked what those objectives are, to find out that every team member is operating to different objectives. Teams do not take the time up front to clearly document objectives. The reason for this is that goal setting is actually often very hard work: controversial, contentious, ambiguous, and messy. Wading through all that can be trying for even the most talented leaders and teams. The tool that Kimberly prescribes provides a systematic approach to help teams navigate through this stormy process. Smart leaders and teams will recognize immediately the value this tool brings to projects in that it provides a clear, short path to arriving at well-defined goals and objectives."

– Matt Schlegel, Director of HW Product Delivery, Palm, Inc.

SCRAPPY TIP: If you don't have clear goals you won't know when you're done. Don't end up in permanent project purgatory! It is up to the project leader to create a grand unified vision of success—what success looks like, feels like, sounds like, tastes like, and smells like. Every single person associated with the project must share a similar hallucination about the end result to which the team is committed in order to make all due speed toward that shared dream.

3 Communication? We've Got Real Work To Do!

Engage in effective, vociferous & unrelenting communication with all stakeholders.

"The major problem with communication is the illusion that it has occurred." – George Bernard Shaw

If you've led even one major project you are undoubtedly aware of the critical link between communication and success. In spite of the fact that project managers spend more than half of their time in meetings and 70-90% of their time communicating, communication is cited as the #2 cause of project failure.[4] Even if you have crystal clear goals and metrics of success, chances are that very few people on your extended team share your clarity. Unfortunately, your lovingly prepared project documents and urgent emails are likely skimmed through—or skipped over—by

---

4. Ref: The Bull Survey (1998), The KPMG Canada Survey (1997), The Chaos Report (1995), The OASIG Study (1995).

your overworked, deadline-driven team. In order to be heard above the roar of the communication blizzard, you must send a clear and compelling message, repeating yourself frequently.

> *"To create change... direct, personal, two-way communication is what makes the difference.... You've got to be out in front of crowds, repeating yourself over and over again, never changing your message, no matter how it bores you."*
>
> – Jack Welch, CEO, General Electric

Welcome to the communication blizzard! We now encounter more information in a single Sunday newspaper than a person in the 17th century encountered in an entire lifetime. On a project of any complexity, the information overload can be downright oppressive.

What project manager doesn't have a big old stack of email in their in-box, a giant pile of unread documents on their desk, and an incessantly flashing "message waiting" light on their voice mail? Paper information is typically "filed" geologically, heaped layer by layer upon the pile until critical project documents are found somewhere in the Mesozoic era. Email tends to become a reminder of the bottomless pit of action items that awaits us if we ever do get caught up. Faced with an onslaught of undifferentiated information and the impossible task of keeping up with it all, we are forced to make tough choices, prioritize, and flat out ignore much of it as a matter of self-preservation.

Our ability to ignore communication isn't at all surprising. If 50% of all the phone calls you received were telemarketers, would you even answer the phone? The human brain is forced to screen out about 99,999,960 out of the ten million bits of information received every second. Only ten to forty bits a second are raised to our conscious awareness.[5] The rest bounces around blissfully in the subconscious where it is quickly forgotten, or at worst creates an amorphous, nagging angst. We humans tend to focus on things that matter to us, things that have meaning. It is exceedingly tempting to seek shelter

---

5. Tor Norretranders, *The User Illusion: Cutting Consciousness Down to Size* (New York: Penguin, 1999).

Chapter 3: Communication? We've Got Real Work To Do!

from the communication storm in the proven strategies of avoidance and procrastination. We get tunnel vision, focus on what's right in front of us, and hope that disaster won't strike as a result.

This snow-blindness can spell difficulty or even disaster for a project. Some examples of the victims of the project communication avalanche follow.

A critical project document, like the goals and metrics of success, is sent to your core team as an attachment to an email message. You ask for their feedback within three days. The predictable response from a blindingly busy team? None. Nada. Zero. What happened? Chances are, most of them never even clicked on the attachment. A few of those who did may send you valuable input, but most of the feedback will fall into the category of "It looks good to me," which translates into "I looked at it and didn't really have time to think much about it" or "I didn't even open the attachment. Who are you kidding?" These are the project *goals*, the committed schedule, the biggest risks, for Pete's sake! It's not like you're asking them to review the boilerplate of a procurement contract.

Critical project documents are stashed on a shared network location, and those seeking the information are referred there with the glib admonition, "It's on the shared drive." I'm all for having shared project folders where the whole team can stash documents and share information. But this is akin to saying that a car is parked somewhere in the city of Tokyo. Unless there's a bit more specificity, and a well-organized file structure, this phrase is extremely entertaining to those who have actually visited the shared drive. Those in the know roll their eyes in amusement at the suggestion that they could actually find the information they seek without burning up a disproportionate amount of precious time that could otherwise be spent knocking off some other, more pressing task.

You can compensate somewhat for these behaviors by calling even more meetings where you all sit around together and review these documents, but that's not a viable option for geographically-dispersed teams. And to be honest, even co-located teams can succumb to over-reliance on electronic forms of communication. Rather than taking the time to walk over and have a conversation about an urgent matter, it's common practice to send an instant message to a teammate who sits only steps away.

Effective Communication. When you think about it, communication is pretty much the only means that we have to lead. While listening is a big part of that, when we do speak, we need to find ways to be heard above the surrounding din. If you want your messages to get through the widespread commotion in most projects, keep it short, keep it relevant, and keep it fun. Poor communication is yet another avoidable cause of project failure. Let's wipe it out in our lifetime!

Graphic 3 shows a simple example of a communications map. This kind of chart typically takes less than 20 minutes to create, and is more communication planning than most people do for a project. I say it's 20 minutes well spent.

Graphic 3: Overly Simplistic Version of a Communications Map

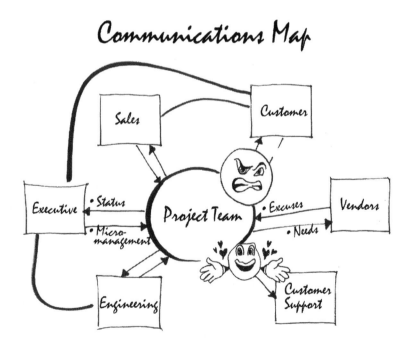

So how can you get your messages to be "the chosen ones" that pierce the consciousness of your team? Here are a few creative approaches that have been proven effective in real-world projects:

Goals. Condense all of the requirements documents and success criteria into a one-page "Project Success Scorecard." (See Chapter 2, "If You Don't Know Where You're Going, Any Road Will Do."). At the risk of sounding repetitive, let me reiterate that success means far more than features delivered on time and under-budget.

Plan. Use a simple flow chart program to create a one-page schedule that represents the high-level timeline of the project from start to finish. Although this is extra work for those of us who are using Microsoft Project and other such scheduling software, a simplified map of how the team will get from the start to a glorious finish helps people to keep the big picture in mind without getting lost in the details of a 937-line Gantt chart. For added impact, highlight areas of greatest risk with clip art like skulls and cross bones, ambulances, and little time bombs. This always makes an impression on executives who tend to notice these sorts of decorations. One thing's for sure, they won't snooze through presentations.

SCRAPPY TIP: *When tracking changes in action item due dates, don't ever change the original dates. Just strike through the obsolete date and let the list of changed dates grow to the point of embarrassment. When an item accumulates enough changes in the due date, it will eventually be obvious to even the most deliberately obtuse that there is a problem.*

Grab Attention. If you are co-located with your team, you have a fabulous opportunity to capture their attention visually. Here are some tactics that, while unconventional—and in some cases uncouth—work like a charm:

- Purchase a life-size cardboard figure of the celebrity of your choice (movie star, political figure, Disney character, whatever) and position them just outside of the team meeting room with the top priority project goals or next big milestone in their hands, paws, or tentacles.

- Create a screensaver that conveys the purpose, goals, and priorities of the project. Make the background picture irresistible so that people can't help but load it onto their computers. (The CEO playing "Whack-A-Mole" is always popular.) Better yet, have your IT Department make this the default screensaver on everyone's PC.

- Post the one-page project timeline—or any other time-critical project communication—inside the restrooms in "strategic" places, places you can be sure people will be looking at for at least a few minutes a day. (Common decency dictates that I not provide any further detail. You know what I mean!)

- Give them a little something "extra" in every email communication. Foster the expectation that your email will entertain as well as inform, via a joke, anecdote, riddle, or inspirational saying. This will increase the likelihood of your messages being read—or at least opened, which is half the battle.

- Use poetry to communicate some critical project details. One unstoppably creative project leader used this technique to increase the on-time attendance at a daily status meeting during a critical juncture. People showed up on time to hear the kick-off poem that captured key issues for the day's meeting.

The "E" in Email. Now let's talk about the global plague that has hit communication in the 21st century. I've had it with project leaders who think that their whole job can be done from a keyboard! I recently helped one of my client companies hire a project manager for a professional services business. The CEO told me they wanted help because "the last three project managers didn't work out." Yeah, that's a big warning sign that something's cookin' in the project management kitchen. It seems that the last project manager was there for a year and had NEVER been to visit a customer. Now, mind you, this was a professional services firm, and the people working on the projects were pretty much always at the customer site. I innocently asked, "How did this person manage the project?" The answer, of course, was email. Paper cuts all over my body just prior to a lemon juice bath couldn't have sent me into more intense convulsions.

A project leader with an addiction to email is destined for trouble. Are you addicted? Here's a quick check-up. Test yourself against these behaviors, all of which I have observed to be epidemic in the stress-fest work environments where I consult:

- The first thing you do when you walk in the door in the morning is check email and clear out your in-box.

- You monitor email all day long.

- You continue to read and respond to email while people are in your office talking with you.

- You send an email to communicate important news instead of holding a meeting.

- You send critical documents that require feedback from busy people as attachments to email and expect them to actually read them.

If even one of these statements describes you, give yourself a good slap across the face, splash water over your stinging skin, and seek help immediately! Surf the web for support groups, call Email-aholics Anonymous, explore your relationship with your higher power, whatever it takes! These are not the characteristics of a highly respected project leader. They are the behavior of an administrator and bureaucrat! Project leaders need to lead, not read, and you can't do that from behind a keyboard.

Now, I know there are plenty of people out there who are going to dash off an email to me protesting that email is a vital project management tool. For years I have been asserting that email is *not* a form of communication, so I'm familiar with the pushback. But in my opinion, email is a data transmission tool. OK, sometimes it is pretty handy, but honestly, don't you think we've gone too far? Too often the "e" in email stands for:

- Evasive – as in a cowardly alternative to a difficult conversation.

- All too **E**asy – as in "the easy way out" of something that deserved a face-to-face chat, or at least a phone call. Or just plain easy for you, and harder for everyone else.

- **E**vil – as in nastygrams that would never have been spoken, and are now preserved forever in some hard drive out there in some server farm.

- And last but not least, **E**fficient, but ineffective.

I'm not even going to try to capture a thorough list of email best practices. Jeff Sandquist already did a great job of that. (Have a look at his web site.[6]) But here are a few tips about some particular burrs under my email-chaffed saddle that I'm just itching to eliminate from the face of the planet.

- Avoid the "hydra" email—an email covering several different topics, each of which requires something from the receivers. Limit each email to one topic, clearly labeled in the subject line, and put "Action Requested" in the subject if you need a response. Winston Churchill used this technique with paper memos, but he was much more blunt, writing the phrase "ACTION REQUIRED THIS DAY" on those concerning urgent matters.

- Don't even think about sending anything remotely sensitive or emotional in an email. If you must write some emotional verbal vomit in an email, at least have the decency and good sense to delete it before sending it. Or send it to yourself. You probably deserve it more than the poor bastard you addressed it to.

- Keep in mind that the person who reads your email gets to imagine your tone of voice and interpret your meaning. No matter how carefully you write, you only control a small percentage of the meaning that will be conveyed. The rest will be supplied by the vivid imagination of the receiver.

---

6. http:/jeffsandquist.com/The10CommandmentsOfEmail.aspx

- Never use BCC. NEVER! If you must secretly let someone else know about some message that you sent, copy yourself and then forward a copy to that other person. For pity's sake, this is for your own good. If the person receiving the BCC hits "Reply All" you will be outted for the sneaky rascal that you probably are.

- Don't play email ping-pong. After a couple of volleys back and forth, pick up the damn phone, or better yet, pay a personal visit to the other person. They probably sit less than ten meters away from you anyhow, and you can probably use the exercise.

All things said and done, it doesn't matter whether you send emails or smoke-signals to convey your messages, just so long as you *communicate!* Communication is absolutely essential for project success, so make sure you communicate early, often, and effectively. It's the leader's job to make sure his message is received and understood. There is no excuse for failing because of an entirely predictable and avoidable problem like communication breakdown. Make no mistake, effective communication is hard work and takes constant vigilance.

4

Hey, It Wasn't Me! It Was "The Others"

Ensure that roles & responsibilities are unmistakably understood and agreed upon by all.

"All organizations are perfectly designed to get the results they get. To get better results, you need to improve the design of the organization."
– Arthur Jones

The very people who are supposed to be leading often abdicate responsibility in mediocre organizations. At every layer of management, these evasive characters somehow avoid committing to anything outside of their minuscule comfort zones and job descriptions. They fog their agreements with weasel words that foreshadow their impending failure to deliver as promised. This behavior is perfectly understandable when we consider that fear of failure is the #1 issue standing in the way of setting goals. Even small goals are dangerous to people who fear the slightest tinge of failure, so don't look to these jokers for any audacious ones. Project leaders can't afford to take this easy way out.

If You're Not Allowed to Fail, Don't Start Anything! Senior executives would love to find a way to get their employees to take greater personal responsibility for the business results that are so vital to their success, even their survival. But many people are afraid to take that kind of responsibility. Instead they hide out, play it safe, and wait for guidance from above. If you're not allowed to fail, you'd better be extremely careful what you start. To be absolutely sure of avoiding failure, best start nothing at all.

Looking to others to make the first move is like cutting a bird apart to figure out how flocking behavior occurs. The answer will never be found there. The person who is capable of making a difference will be found in the mirror, not above us in the org chart. For people willing to cop to their own contribution to both the problem and the solution, possibilities abound. All it takes is the courage to risk failure and a willingness to be uncomfortable.

Funnily enough, avoiding responsibility works pretty well in some corporate environments. Some companies value being inoffensive over being effective. In these tepid bastions of sloth, courageous leadership, clear commitments, and unmistakable accountability are a bit of a lost art. More than a few professionals have made a pretty good career for themselves by waiting for others to stick their heads up out of the trenches. The last person with their head still intact is king! It's de-evolution at its finest. If you've chosen this path in the past but now have the burning desire to transform yourself into a more responsible corporate citizen, you've come to the right place.

No Confidence Is Required—Only Absolute Commitment.
Responsible project leaders make clear commitments to which they can be held accountable. Sure, this makes them an easy target for the CAVE people we've mentioned before, as well as for the vast majority of humans who make a habit of criticizing, condemning, and complaining about pretty much everything. No matter. Scrappy Project Managers boldly declare, "You can count on me," and plaster their target on their cubicle wall with courage and conviction.

But courage and conviction can be a double-edged sword. Sometimes, commitments must be made without all the details. Unexpected distractions might arise that could make it difficult or impossible to keep a promise. And our sometimes overly-ambitious goals will involve the distinct possibility of failure—which is no reason to avoid them, mind you. Certainly, attempts at quantum leaps carry considerable risk, but there is also tremendous upside potential. We frequently underestimate what we're capable of, so lean toward over-committing.

People who dare to commit to more than they think they're capable of are a menace to mediocrity. They stand in stark contrast to those who survive while managing the business to a slow, steady decline, what I call a "go out of business as slowly as possible" approach.

Every project seems a bit overly ambitious at the beginning. If you intend to lead a wildly successful project, you'd better have people willing to take on more than they think they can handle. "Dive in and invent the water on the way down!" one inspiring coach told me. I prefer someone who will take on a challenge fully and work like hell to make it happen over some namby-pamby double-talker any day.

Defining Roles and Responsibilities. Working in a matrix organization, as many of us do, means we're responsible for delivering results that require intense cross-functional coordination, not to mention the cooperation of individuals who may report to several functional managers. Team members rarely report to the project leader, in spite of decades of experience indicating that important projects would benefit greatly if they did. As a result, many projects muddle along without clearly defined roles for various team members. Sometimes people aren't even quite sure who the leader is. Like a body without a head, the team lurches fitfully toward some hazy destination, unsure of who's doing what. Many projects include people from different functional areas and at different levels of seniority, further complicating the relationships. And people can hide out in these fuzzy roles, avoiding responsibility.

Project management training often refers to creating a Responsibility Allocation Matrix, or RAM. I rather favor a visual "one throat to choke" approach, a one-page visual of inescapably clear roles and responsibilities without wiggle room. A Project Team Org Chart like that recommended by Michael McGrath in *Setting the P.A.C.E. in Product Development* can clarify the relationship of team members and who is leading the charge in each key area.[7] (See an example in Graphic 4.)

---

7. M. McGrath, *Setting the P.A.C.E. in Product Development,* (Burlington, MA: Elvesier, 1996), pp. 54-58.

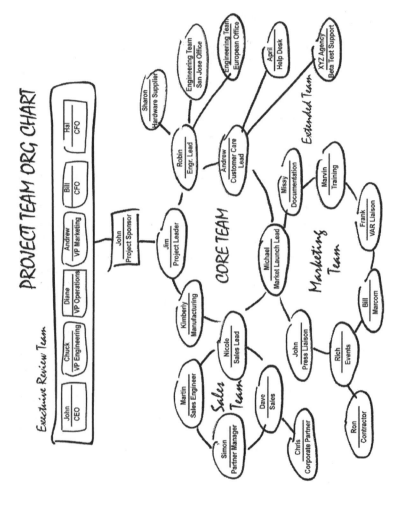

Graphic 4: Bare Minimum Project Team Org Chart

    Chapter 4: Hey, It Wasn't Me! It Was "The Others"

Regardless of the positional titles of the people involved, this org chart focuses on the roles of individuals in the project and their relationship to other project team members. The Project Team Org Chart has no dotted line reporting relationships or crisscrossing matrices where people report to multiple managers. It unmistakably aligns goals and roles, at least for the duration of the project. By publishing this chart to the team, their functional managers, and beyond, you establish an expectation of functional area leadership, teamwork, and accountability to the project that is stronger than a position in some outdated hierarchical staffing diagram. Typical org charts are quite useful when you're going to be late for work and you want to know who to call, but they don't show how projects happen in most companies. The Project Team Org Chart can easily and completely replace the traditional Responsibility Allocation Matrix with just a few bullets next to each person's name indicating key areas of responsibility.

You don't need a slick diagram posted on the company intranet to achieve this kind of clarity. Sometimes "good enough" is. For co-located teams, a simple hand-drawn chart hung where all members can see it is plenty good enough. While the core team can probably get by without such a diagram, this kind of chart is more important for people who are peripherally involved with the team. They are the ones most likely to be unsure of each person's role. Once everyone involved in any way with the project clearly understands roles, the pace of progress quickens and the frequency of the blame game slackens.

Why bother making your own team org chart? Generally, companies are not as simplistic as the hierarchical organization charts drawn to describe them. Take a look at one and you'll probably be able to discern who's earning the highest salary, but I doubt that you'll see anything remotely resembling how work in your project gets done. Traditional functional org charts contain little indication of the rich and complex working relationships most business results depend on. In today's fast-moving global business environment, projects cut across functional areas and teammates aren't related by any formal organizational ties.

Failure By Design: The Politics of Tuna Sandwiches. The matrix organization is a frustrating reality for most project leaders. The problem isn't necessarily the matrix organization itself, but its implementation. Like so many things in life, it sounds perfectly fine in theory—but in practice, working in a matrix organization is less than sub-optimal. Project managers are pitted against (so-called) functional managers in a struggle over resources, in pursuit of what are frequently different priorities.

I've never been a slave to the status quo, so when I am asked how project managers can be effective in a matrix organization, I'm not necessarily quick to answer. To me, that question is like inquiring into the sexual orientation of a rock, or the political affiliation of a tuna sandwich. We need to start asking the meta-question, "What organizational structures best support project and business success?" It's time to take the red pill, Neo!

The fact is that traditional company structures no longer serve the needs of the rapidly-changing world in which businesses operate. Today, creating successful outcomes on most projects requires not only a combination of cross-functional talents, but also the support of suppliers, customers, contractors, and alliance partners. All of these people are critical to success, and all of them are conspicuously absent from those neat and tidy tree diagrams that pass for org charts. So project managers are inserted, and expected to manage a patchwork quilt team sewn from bits and pieces found across the organization. We succeed not because of, but in spite of, the organizational structures our teams must navigate.

Ossified Org Charts in a Gumby World. Traditional organizational structures are hard to change, but business needs are changing quickly these days. Whole industries come and go in the time it used to take to design and produce a single product. Next quarter's project might require completely different people, skills, and technology than the last one. One of my favorite cartoon characters as a child was Gumby, a green, rubbery, bendable guy with an equally pliable horse named Pokey. To be successful in today's business environment, we need to be like Gumby—flexible and adaptable to the ever-evolving landscape in which we operate.

Wouldn't it be nice if our organizational structures could shape-shift as quickly as the challenges we face—not just once every couple of years, like some corporate reorganization cycles, but truly adapting to the business needs in real time? Surely a more flexible structure makes sense, and some types of organizations do a bit of this. But why isn't a readily reconfigurable organizational structure more commonplace? Why aren't companies that can nimbly shift to optimally meet customer and business needs more common in our corporate landscape?

The Titanic Collapse. One reason is that project managers somehow make the existing mess work. My other guess is that it's because people love their titles. One VP of HR confided to me that when mergers, acquisitions, or reorganizations occur, the biggest obstacle to creating the new organizational structure is people's attachment to their titles. As Patrick Lencioni noted in *The Five Dysfunctions of a Team* (I was surprised to find that there were only five!), concerns about status and ego dominate in the absence of a shared vision and compelling team goals. Lest you think this is just a business issue, pick up *Collapse: How Societies Choose to Fail or Succeed*. In this frightening book, Jared Diamond points out that leaders of civilizations facing a looming catastrophe tend to occupy themselves with building bigger and more expensive monuments to themselves rather than tackle the root causes of the decline. (Did somebody mutter global warming?)

Instead of making necessary changes that will benefit the community as a whole, those in positions of power tend to be satisfied with a first class cabin on their sinking ship. Perhaps this is the fate of rigid corporate structures as well. Rather than risking their place in the pecking order by establishing a more flexible structure, most business leaders will likely stave off the inevitable as long as possible, and then fade into oblivion to be studied along with the dead shells of their corporations, like so many Mayan ruins.

The Headlight of an Oncoming Train? I can sense the looks of futility and the shrugging shoulders around the world as I write. What can be done? If whole civilizations have gone extinct rather than change, can we really expect to change the way companies are structured? Don't slit your wrists yet! It's not all doom and gloom out there. There are leaders willing to sacrifice their personal interest in favor of the greater good. I just can't think of any at the moment.

While we might not be able to squeeze time in our workday to change the whole organization, I believe we can at least create a more effective environment for the people on our teams. Here are my top four tips for making the organizational structure irrelevant, at least as it relates to our projects:

* Demonstrate to your people that they can make a meaningful difference by contributing to your project. Present people with a worthy cause and they will lose interest in status, ego, and the hierarchy. People join companies because of their reputation or promise, but they stay because they believe that their jobs have meaning, their relationships matter, and that their dreams can come true.

* Make it your business to learn what each person cares deeply about, and figure out how that aligns with supporting the project. Make your project the means by which people can fulfill their dreams and it won't matter what their title is on the org chart. People contribute more when it's easy to see that their contributions count. When a clear line-of-sight exists between a person's actions and their impact on the project, they will be far more motivated to extend themselves and make a positive difference.

* Provide recognition for contributions to the project that far exceed any reward that the functional organization offers. Contrary to popular belief, appreciation is not expressed by the money in someone's paycheck. It's best demonstrated by the sincere appreciation of a job well done. Recognizing and appreciating people in a way that dwarfs their typical positive feedback system shouldn't be difficult in most organizations. True appreciation is a rather scarce commodity in most business environments. I recently asked a senior manager whether he felt appreciated by his company and he said, "They don't make it too terribly painful to work here." Gee, it should be easy to improve on that! People do what is rewarded, and if working on your project is the most gratifying part of their job, believe me, it won't matter much how or whether they report to you. They'll be more than happy to support the project goals if you show them a shred of appreciation!

- Finally, create your own project team org chart that makes existing ones irrelevant, at least as far as the project is concerned. No one looks at the standard corporate org chart anyhow, and in some organizations it's such a well kept secret that only the recruiters working for the competition have a copy.

No one can give you what you deny yourself. Don't be a victim! There are plenty of things outside of your control, but defining clear roles for your team is not one of them. Do whatever you need to do to make the relationships in the project team more important to team members than the rigid reporting relationships in the existing company structure. Your project team can be your people's "first team" regardless of the corporate morass that surrounds them.

Duct Tape for the Traditional Org Chart. If a taillight is broken and needs to be fixed quickly, crafty drivers who wish to avoid a traffic ticket will get themselves a roll of duct tape that will hold things together until the damage can be properly repaired. Available in 15 eye-popping colors, it can even do a pretty good impression of a real taillight from a distance. But make no mistake, it still looks wrecked. And as handy as duct tape is, it's a short-term fix.

Despite their owners' best intentions, some cars will still have that shabby-looking duct tape taillight years later. You can't see your taillight when you're driving, so there's no real pressure to get it fixed. What's behind us isn't important. In the absence of clear roles for each person on the team, the project manager ends up as the duct tape holding together the dangling bits of an outdated organizational structure. Don't settle for a patched-together team of ill-defined relationships and responsibilities. Roll your own!

The Drum Circle—An Old World Metaphor for 21st Century Teams. If you've never played in a drum circle you really owe it to yourself to find one in your local area and check it out. It's a fabulous metaphor for shared responsibility in project teams in chaotic environments. Many drum circles exist as a self-organizing system that appears to lack a recognized leader or clear roles. In spite of this, they are a fascinating demonstration of achieving complex outcomes in groups of people who enjoy immense freedom in a loosely-defined framework.

A drum circle happens when people sit down together with an intention to make music. Players tend to join or depart as they wish, and pretty much do their own thing without guidance from a central authority. Frequently, there is little or no discussion of what will be played. Drummers enjoy the freedom of creating their roles based on their experience, their instrument of choice, and their real-time interaction with the other players. Sometimes it starts off very messy, like the front end of an ill-defined project. As more people noisily join in, they manage to find a way to whack, boom, or bang out some kind of rhythm that makes sense to them. The group lurches fitfully for a while as people find their place in the mayhem. Eventually someone will start laying down a beat that others voluntarily pick up. Then ... BAM! The whole drum circle is "in the groove" and going for the ride of their lives! These are non-stop, meditative, and hypnotic stretches of jamming, which can range from ten minutes to two hours or more. You've just got to experience the adrenaline rush to understand what a thrill it is to be part of this heaving mass of humanity and vibration.

Seemingly without effort, players come to agreement on what kind of music to create. Inevitably, a core group of players will establish a solid base beat so that others can ornament the music with something more intricate. As the music unfolds, individuals manage to solo without stepping on someone else's solo.

Changes occur during the playing, but it's usually so loud that there's no point in talking about it. Changing the beat, picking up the pace, or working out the parts happens through a subtle combination of eye contact and musical cues. Most amazing of all, this throbbing force of nature often manages to come to a breath-taking simultaneous stop by mutual agreement.

So how can an avalanche of sound and adrenaline like this be controlled? It can't. Much like a project team's work, it can only be shaped and guided by mutual agreement, cooperation, and compromise.

There are some terrific metaphors here for leading and creating role clarity in a diverse project team:

• Choose players who fit together.

• Make sure the right instruments are in the circle.

• As a leader, play an instrument that can be heard by others. A weak voice will be lost in the chaos.

• Lay down a clear and steady beat as the foundation that supports the others.

• Ensure that everyone can make eye contact and use body language and facial expression to communicate. Email just won't cut it in a fast-moving, self-organizing drum circle.

• Lead in the direction that the team is already heading. If the beat is moving in a new direction that works, go with it.

• If you do decide to jump in front and overtly lead by conducting, you'd better get their agreement to follow. Otherwise, you'll just look silly waving your arms around directing while the band plays on, oblivious to your leadership.

The rhythm of projects is much more complicated these days. Project teams are no longer well-defined, orderly groups of people playing clear roles in deference to a project leader. If you want to lead effectively in today's project environment you might want to get yourself a djembe and drop in on a drum circle to see what you can learn about self-organizing systems like this. Not only is it eye-opening, it's a whole lot of fun! For more insight on drum circles, search out one of the many great books by Arthur Hull (http://www.drumcircle.com).

Unclear roles are just the start of a mudslide of project problems. If people don't clearly understand their place in the organization, they might assume that they don't matter. If they don't know how important their role is to your project, they might sit idly by waiting for someone else to do something about the pressing issues of the day. Eventually, they find other, more gratifying places to make a difference. One friend who was languishing in a quagmire of functionally-siloed bureaucrats set the ultimate example. Realizing that it is easier to start a whole new organization from scratch than to change an existing one, she quit and started her own company. In helping her create a business plan we described the org chart of the team needed to make her business successful. Believe me, there isn't any nonsense like permanent titles or silly tree diagrams! Our plan serves the needs of the business first and leaves the ego-centric hierarchical structure to the 21st century Mayans.

5 Why Plan? Let's Just Get Moving!

Create viable plans & schedules that enjoy the team's hearty commitment.

"A carelessly-planned project takes three times longer to complete than expected; a carefully planned project takes only twice as long."
– Golub's Law

Common sense says that when working on a project with results that matter, teams should agree on a plan of how to achieve the goals, consider what might go wrong, and make sure everyone who needs to deliver results is committed to doing what needs to be done to make it happen. Here's a bit of news about the real world of project management: Common sense isn't common practice. It's not even common knowledge. Most so-called common sense is so obvious that people think it "goes without saying." Unfortunately, *nothing* goes without saying!

Given a choice, most people will either under-plan or not plan at all. Many crises experienced during a project can be traced back to poor planning in the early phases. Most projects are under severe time constraints, so planning must be accomplished quickly in order to meet those challenging deadlines. Planning never feels like the right thing to do. When there is a mountain of work piled in front of you and you're already late, the last thing you feel like doing is sitting down to set clear goals, clarify assumptions, and lay out milestones, owners, and due dates for deliverables. As a result, projects routinely suffer from under-planning. This is especially true of projects led by novices or by people occupying the position of a project manager but lacking the discipline of professional project management.

How do inexperienced people end up at the helm of critical projects? Some execs assume that any sensible person can be an adequate project leader (even extremely adequate!), so they put the fate of a critical project in the hands of someone who will spend more time wringing them than helping the team. These people may sit in the chair of a project leader, but make no mistake—they aren't real leaders. They're often smug amateurs, the kind of people who carry around a clipboard and check things off. These guys just jump in and work like hell to get the job done, skipping over silly little things like clarifying success criteria or creating the buy-in and support of key stakeholders. Just a smidgeon of planning, a pinch of risk mitigation, a dash of clear roles and responsibilities can put you head and shoulders above most project managers.

Plan? We've Got Real Work to Do! The first temptation that any project manager must overcome is the tendency to start working on the project before the goals are clear. After all, during the planning process no code is written, no sheet metal cut, no circuits laid out, no products built, shipped, or even sold. (OK, sometimes products are sold before they are even developed, but we don't want to go there, do we?) The temptation is to get the team busy, busy, busy, working on "stuff" rather than planning effectively.

It's been said, "Fail to plan and plan to fail," but planning just isn't the kind of activity that garners attention, accolades, and appreciation. The planning process can even seem like a barrier to "real work." Activity can be a seductive substitute for progress. Human beings are notoriously prone to shortcutting the planning process and jumping right into activities that may make little or no contribution to the desired end goal. It can be months before anyone notices because being busy feels so good! It passes the time, and makes it seem like we're making headway even if we're just racing around full speed ahead in a great big circle. Like a salmon swimming tirelessly against a mighty, rushing stream, little progress may be made in spite of a tremendous investment of effort.

Every hour of planning saves about a day of wasted time and effort.[8] It's simple, and yet, given a choice, most people will do little or no planning whatsoever. What's up with that? Think about it. When you're planning, it doesn't look like any work is getting done. You're just ... planning!

One reason why teams are reluctant to plan sufficiently is because they know that things inevitably change. Knowing that a plan is susceptible to sometimes massive changes, most people would prefer knocking a few tasks off of their individual task list to spending valuable time drawing up a project plan that might be changed at any moment.

Every team member needs to realize that planning is real work, deserves time and attention, and can be of far greater importance than rushing headlong into the project. This realization alone, however, does not mean that things will go smoothly. Remember our dead moose and our lost whale? Well, they aren't the only mammals endangered by projects that are out of control. The most amazingly hideous things can and do happen on projects, and many of them can be avoided—or mitigated relatively painlessly—with a small investment in the planning process.

When a team is in chaos, and people are starting to wander into the tidal zone, what they need more than anything is a little time to think. All a project leader needs to do is call a meeting and insist that planning be done. If we call a halt to the frenzy and put some sensible plans in place, then there's at least a chance that any further activity will result in real progress towards the goals.

---

8. Steve McConnell, *Software Project Survival Guide*. (Redmond, WA: Microsoft Press,1998), p. 36.

Schedules Shouldn't Be Found in the Fiction Section of the Library. One of the most important parts of many projects is the committed project schedule. Schedules can frequently be the soft underbelly of project planning. The most meticulously detailed Gantt chart can mask a multitude of uncertainties. Why are schedules so tough to plan? Because most projects are late even before they start. Frequently it's because they should have been started months earlier, mind you, but until time travel is invented I'm not taking on that challenge! And some projects just pop into existence with little warning, landing on the fast track of "Get it done ASAP."

Once a project is in motion many teams can be loath to spend the time required to create a realistic, fact-based schedule they can stake their reputation on. Even if you can get a team to step back and take a whack at a decent schedule, most of the resulting plans are unrealistic from the get go. In my experience, the most significant causes of hideous performance against schedules are:

- Human brains are just plain lousy at making estimates, and that includes estimating task durations in project schedules.

- Bottom-up scheduling methods pay too little attention to handoffs and integration points.

- Executives and project leaders engage in "The Lying Game."

- Teams wait until the schedule slips before intervening.

- Lessons learned from the previous project aren't applied to the next project.

You don't need to be a fortune-teller to know that pretty much all schedules using single-number estimates for durations and due dates are wrong. It's been well known for decades that using weighted average ranges, including best case to worst case estimates, enable far more accurate schedule predictions than those popularized by software programs like Microsoft Project. You can con a sucker into committing to an impossible deadline, but you can't con him into meeting it.

Critical Path Hot Potato. Fortunately, many supposedly "time-critical" projects aren't. Very few amount to a death sentence for the project or the company if the schedule slips. But occasionally a project deadline is more than an arbitrarily established ruse to "motivate" the team to "go the extra mile." There are times when a schedule absolutely must be met in a predictable way, without fail. That's when you need to cut through the all too prevalent web of lies and self-delusion. Most schedules earn smirks and derision from the team far before it is obvious that they were never more than a grand illusion. When you need a schedule that you can take to the bank, it's time to cut the B.S., pull out your scrappy scheduling skills, and unmask the naked and shivering truth.

In these circumstances, it's unwise to placate executives who demand an unrealistic schedule that will ultimately slip week by week to the original realistic date. Grow a backbone! Don't say it's not possible; that instantly blows your credibility with executives who must deliver critical business results. But do have an open and honest conversation about what it's going to take to make it happen. Don't let the critical path hot potato land in your lap! Take sensible steps in creating your schedule, or it's déjà vu all over again for you and your project team.

It's easy enough to say and mighty difficult to do. Regardless of company size, executives seem united in their lack of understanding of the interdependency of the quality, features, budget, and schedule of a project. Understandably driven by business needs to announce, launch, and ship products around certain market-driven dates, they often appear to be unreasonable, even irrational. A project leader may spend hours, days, or weeks creating a detailed project plan, including detailed timelines, resources, risks, and mitigation, only to have an executive arbitrarily tell them to "cut two months off of the schedule" without changing the scope or adding resources. It's at this point that the difference between a Scrappy Project Manager and someone merely filling the chair of a project manager becomes clear. Nodding compliantly like some kind of bobble-head doll just doesn't do your team justice.

Time to Think. People tend to think that they know what to do, and don't need to write it all down. It can be very satisfying to charge ahead. But consider this: most people forget at least 50% of what they hear at a meeting the minute they walk out the door, and fully 80% within two months of the meeting. The faintest pencil is more persistent than the strongest memory. As a project leader, you can best enable your team to avoid this predictable and avoidable pitfall by insisting that they follow this simple project planning process:

1. STOP!
2. THINK! (at least for a nanosecond)
3. Then, and ONLY then, ACT!

Attacked by Plan-ophobia. Believe me, people with adrenal glands working overtime are not going to think of this option, but they desperately need to spend time thinking and planning—individually and collectively—before tackling the next pile of work. The best way to do this is to have a set of guiding principles for project planning and stick to them.

Fearless project leaders insist on appropriate planning even when the mobocracy clamors for mindless motion. Liking it is optional; doing it is mandatory. Sometimes asking your team to spend a day hip deep in the planning process takes real guts. Naysayers will claim that there is real work to be done, and those who are uncomfortable or inexperienced with project planning will need your step-by-step guidance to grope their way through the process.

When I ask about project plans, sometimes a Microsoft Project Gantt chart is thrust into my sweaty little hands. Don't mistake a Gantt chart for a project plan. Microsoft Project was invented to make a messy and chaotic process look tidy and well defined. This is a dangerous illusion, and may lull your team into a warm, soft koosh ball of security that will turn into a porcupine right about the time your project *should* be finishing up, which it won't be. Most Gantt charts look like a map of downtown Tokyo, and are equally incomprehensible. I find that a one-page flow chart with swimlanes for each functional area of the project like the one in Graphic 5 makes a lot more sense. It's also a lot easier for people to follow than a fancy Gantt chart that can only be printed on E-size paper and could be mistaken for the circuit design of some next generation CPU. Of course, you will want to have more detailed work breakdown structures and schedules too, but this bird's eye view keeps everyone rowing in the same general direction.

Scrappy Swimlane High Level Overview

~Jan   ~Apr   ~July   ~Oct

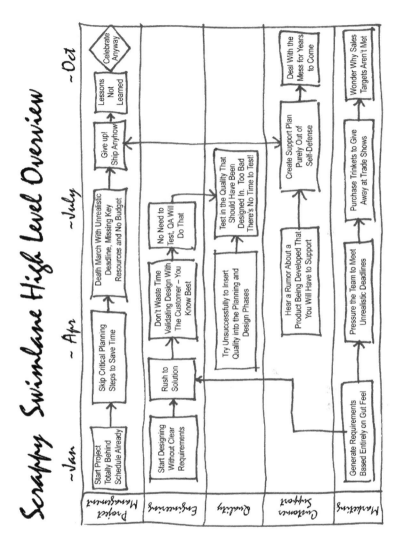

Project Management
- Start Project Totally Behind Schedule Already
- Skip Critical Planning Steps to Save Time
- Death March With Unrealistic Deadline, Missing Key Resources and No Budget
- Give up! Ship Anyhow
- Lessons Not Learned
- Celebrate Anyway

Engineering
- Start Designing Without Clear Requirements
- Rush to Solution
- Don't Waste Time Validating Design With The Customer – You Know Best

Quality
- No Need to Test, QA Will Do That
- Test in the Quality That Should Have Been Designed In. Too Bad There's No Time to Test!

Customer Support
- Try Unsuccessfully to Insert Quality into the Planning and Design Phases
- Hear a Rumor About a Product Being Developed That You Will Have to Support
- Create Support Plan Purely Out of Self-Defense
- Deal With the Mess for Years to Come

Marketing
- Generate Requirements Based Entirely on Gut Feel
- Pressure the Team to Meet Unrealistic Deadlines
- Purchase Trinkets to Give Away at Trade Shows
- Wonder Why Sales Targets Aren't Met

Graphic 5: High Level Project Flowchart with Swimlanes

Even though I grudgingly admit that I do create monstrous Microsoft Project schedules for big projects, I never show those schedules to executives or to people peripherally involved in the project. They're just too confusing to read and too difficult to understand. Instead, I take the time to create an artistic interpretation of the actual detailed schedule in a flow chart form. This flow chart is a one-page map of how the team will move from the start to the finish of the project. It focuses on the critical path and other likely suspects in the competition to be the critical path (because sometimes the critical path tends to jump around a bit like a tourist on a blazingly hot Mexican beach). This kind of visual makes it much easier to have the conversations with execs about the gremlins threatening the schedule completion date. It keeps the attention on the most important aspects of the project instead of diluting attention with the hundreds of different tasks in Project or an Excel spreadsheet, the most frequently used project planning tool.

SCRAPPY TIP: *The planning document is the least of it. The hands-on involvement of key stakeholders in the planning is the most valuable part of the process. Don't settle for a hollow plan that looks neat and tidy. Insist on meaningful planning dialogues with the people who will be doing the work.*

Planning saves time, it doesn't waste it. It will never feel like the right thing to spend time on when you're super busy! Don't wait to "feel" like you have time to plan. Plan with the future in mind. Sometimes project planning focuses too much on the past, on what happened last time, on what has been possible up until this point. This is like driving 200 km/hour with your eyes glued to the rearview mirror! Only slightly better are those who are driving with their eyes focused on the windshield—focusing only on the immediate concerns of the day. Their plans amount to "doing their best." When someone tells me they are doing their best, I worry! Projects can fail quite nicely when everyone is doing their best. In the words of Winston Churchill, one of my favorite leadership role models, "Sometimes doing your best is not enough. Sometimes you must do what is required!" Yeah, that's right, Winston.

Safety in Confusion. Not everyone wants to avoid pandemonium, mind you. There's safety in chaos. It's easier to hide there. As the project plan and status become more inspectable, there's increased accountability. Certain people will become uncomfortable with this increased visibility, as they are stripped of the obscuring cloak of chaos. Sometimes the emperor really is naked, so naturally he starts covering his naughty bits! As a project leader, your role is to ensure that enough planning occurs to effectively deliver results regardless of how busy people are. My motto is, "Just enough planning to optimize results. Not a drop more! ... but not a drop less either."

Some people even become addicted to the adrenaline rush of "fire-fighting," scurrying around in a tizzy extinguishing the latest project-threatening blazes bursting into flames around them. Beware: Firefighters carry matches! Don't encourage these pyromaniacs by paying them too much attention.

It's tough to keep your head with all of the commotion that goes on during a project, so it's helpful to have some guiding principles to follow when things get murky. A recipe doesn't make cookies, but it's a start. Here's a one-page recipe to planning that I have been using for years to guide me through treacherous waters. (See Chapter 6, "Risk? What Could Possibly Go Wrong?") This recipe helps me stay focused on what's important when stress rises like the mercury in a thermometer in the Arizona desert and drives all of the blood from my brain. When I'm not thinking straight I can follow the recipe and avoid adding to my own problems by skipping over the basics. I don't follow this precisely, of course, but at least when I depart from it I do so thoughtfully, not by accidentally forgetting some important part of the planning process. Don't use my recipe, for Pete's sake! Make one that's your very own that suits you and the way you work.

SCRAPPY PROJECT MANAGEMENT
Get It Done Guide

WHO WHAT WHY NOT? HOW

• Team Org Chart

• Communication Map/Stakeholders

• Charter
• Scorecard
• Priorities

Priorites
#1-Heart
#2-Lungs
#3-Kidneys

• Risks & Obstacles

PEOPLE PLANS GOALS
ACTIONS!

• Project Plans
• Integrated Schedule

Copyright Wiefling Consulting 2007

Great chefs don't need a recipe, but good cooks can cook like a great chef with the right recipe and the discipline to follow it.

Baking Your Project Pie. Follow this recipe and taste success in your project.

1. Start with WHO. Identify key stakeholders and their interests, and the team responsible for getting the project done.

2. Prioritize the stakeholders, and use their voices to drive choices in the project planning and execution. Ask, "What will each stakeholder be saying when this project is wildly successful?"

3. Use the insights gained from the WHO stakeholder analysis to develop the "WHAT." Create a success scorecard that captures clear and vivid metrics of success, and the absolute minimum requirements for considering this project successfully complete.

4. WHY NOT? Identify everything standing in your way: risks, obstacles, self-limiting assumptions and beliefs.

5. Separate items that are "gravity" (out of your control) from those you can do something about. Prioritize those that you can control, then kill them off before they grow into monster problems, too big to tackle successfully.

6. Put the whole essence of what the project is into a one-page project flow chart. Even better, if possible, put the whole thing on an index card. It's all people have time to read anyhow!

7. HOW? Create detailed plans and schedules sufficient to get started, and review and revise those frequently along the way, as change is an absolute certainty in most projects.

The next time you're looking down the barrel of another killer project, you will be well served if you pause and reflect before diving into the fray. In the middle of the madness, surface for a look around before digging into the pile of work that awaits you. Cling to what you know works. In spite of the many distractions, Scrappy Project Managers must create an island of clarity in a sea of chaos. We must ensure that everyone shares the same vivid hallucination about what project success looks like, sounds like, tastes like, feels like, and smells like. A set of project planning guidelines like those above can be a useful reminder of key areas that are important to the success of your team. Follow the principles, or depart from them thoughtfully, no matter how you feel at the moment. Remember, professional project leaders do what needs to be done, whether or not they feel like it. Not everyone will like this kind of disciplined approach, but your team deserves a shot at success—and it's up to you to keep your head, stay on solid ground, and guide anyone mucking about in the rip tides safely to shore.

6 Risk? What Could Possibly Go Wrong?

Mitigate big, hairy, abominable risks & implement innovative accelerators.

"Real boats rock." – Frank Herbert

The most frequent mistake that project teams make with regard to risk management might surprise you. The #1 mistake in project risk management is to identify risks but do nothing about them. I've found that people contribute quite enthusiastically to the long list of how the project might meet with disaster. But it's rare that they'll devote as much attention to tracking, avoiding, and mitigating these risks. The risks lurking about are identified and tracked in a well-organized document that is reviewed, approved, stapled, and filed, then never again sees the light of day. In retrospect, it's completely predictable. After all, the team barely has time to do the minimum required of them without addressing possible problems that only might occur. Chances are that, once created, the risk list won't even be read again, let alone used to drive decisions and behavior. Oh, it might be handy during the post-project review, as it could save time re-listing everything that went wrong. This is what we call "documenting your demise."

Very few teams have the time, money, or people to actually do something about anything but the most gargantuan threats to their project success. You could appeal to your executive sponsor, if you have one, but some execs have no imagination for disaster. Incapable of visualizing the land mines that might exist in the treacherous landscape of a typical project, they innocently ask, "What could possibly go wrong?" while flatly denying your requests for more people, more money, and more time. I especially like the helpless shrug with hands outstretched sometimes used while shooting down my perfectly reasonable and well-supported requests. It's small comfort at the end of the project to find that the top three issues that derailed your team topped the risk management spreadsheet. Yet, this is indeed what happens again and again, like some amnesiac dance.

Of course, it's not always the biggest or most obvious risks that stop us cold in our tracks. I've seen projects stalled within centimeters of the finish line for lack of a single screw or a user manual. Have a delicate instrument that requires careful handling? "Hey, we forgot the customized shipping box!" Oops!!! Better hope that the post office carries something in your size. From my stint as a reliability engineer, I happen to know that most packages are dropped from a height of three feet or more dozens of times during shipping, so hopefully your product's not fragile. Bring on the bubble wrap! (Yes, this stuff really happens, usually in small companies running so fast that people are a few blocks ahead of their brains throughout most of the project. But it happens in big companies too, so stay vigilant!)

Even worse is the track record of teams in considering and acting upon possible accelerators—the potential upside available in the sea of possibilities in which the project swims. When teams are in the midst of a struggle for mere survival, the last thing that crosses their minds is how things could go even better than expected. But that is exactly what the best teams do when considering risk. They ask, "What could go better than expected? What could go right. . . and how can we make sure that it does? How could we get lucky in this project?" Keep in mind what other successful people have learned: the harder you work the luckier you get.

The Bad Project Management Olympics. Project management gaffes extend far beyond killing moose, losing whales, or thwarting bridge builders. We wish this kind of happenstance was a rare occurrence in an otherwise blemish-free profession, the stuff of the "Bad Project Management Olympics," only showing its ugly face every 4 years or so. Sadly, it seems to be much more commonplace. Maybe I suck as a project manager, but in my own lamentable experiences, these kinds of surprising lapses are a pretty widespread problem. On one project, we made so many inconceivable missteps that one day some of us actually turned to one another and asked, "Is this just a particularly lengthy string of bad luck, or are we all truly incompetent?" The tragedy of errors (there was nothing comic about it after a while) included the following fumbles:

- We sent a drawing for a sheet metal part to a shop to be prototyped, and they called to ask, "Which Rev. A do you want us to make? We've got two." You can never have too many "Rev. A" drawings, right?

- We sent the gold master of our software to our hard disk duplicator to have hundreds of hard disk drives duplicated with the operating system for a critical production run, only to find out that old bugs resurfaced because we'd compiled an outdated version of the code. Oh, and we repeated this boo-boo several times. We were going full speed ahead. . . in circles!

- We couldn't get our plastic parts painted the same color twice. We flew to Asia to check out the situation on the ground. In the back room was a collection of unsealed cans of our extra special custom paint. . . evaporating. Want a slightly different color? Just wait a couple of days.

- We spent hours trying to nail down the packaging requirements with our Fortune 500 partner when, seething with thinly disguised frustration, they finally inquired, "Why don't you just look at the sample we provided you two months ago?" The wayward sample had been given to our VP of Engineering. When I tracked him down he pulled it out from under his desk. He'd never thought to give it to the team working on the project. (I'm not sure, but I think he was keeping his pet hamster in there.)

Considering that this was a "bet the company" project, we'd all hoped for better performance from others and from ourselves. Unfortunately, when human beings are bone-weary, haggard, and worn to a thread, performance is negatively impacted. All we could do is hang our heads and mutter, "I see stupid people."

Success Staring in the Face of Failure. In this particular case, the story had a happy ending. In spite of all of these setbacks, we managed to snatch success from the jaws of defeat. The turning point was a blood ritual of sorts, where we committed to our goals and to each other.

One day the entire exhausted team sat in a conference room and swore an oath that we were going to make this project successful no matter what. We brainstormed risks and accelerators and created a high-risk schedule that the team committed to in the face of almost certain failure. Then we pulled every creative trick in the book to stick to that seemingly impossible schedule. Of course we made a second schedule that was much less risky to show to the execs and customers. But we kept working to the unrealistic schedule, knowing that surprises would most definitely eat away at the margin we had between our target and what we had promised our customer. This approach is based on Eli Goldratt's "Theory of Constraints," a systems approach to project schedules. It's more like "timeline risk analysis" than scheduling, and it's the only way I know to create predictable schedules that get done on time, besides just shipping whatever happens to be finished by the due date.

Through a combination of relentless hard work and the occasional miracle, we managed to deliver a day or two earlier than promised. It was a tremendous triumph for the team and the entire company was spared what could have been a terminal failure, at least for the moment. What a rush! I personally feel very fortunate to have been able to work with the extraordinary team that pulled this off, and still feel a tingling sensation when I fondly recall that blissful moment. As you might imagine, the following week we were on to the next impossible project, but it was a pleasant couple of nanoseconds.

The Bottom Line. There have been several shocking incidents over the years when a predicted risk issue—one that we all knew was a potentially leviathan problem—hit us like a ton of bricks. We were completely blindsided by the problem that was on our risk list. We blinked bemusedly at one another. We had all been scrambling to deal with more immediate catastrophes, and we had allocated absolutely no bandwidth to watching out for the next wave of calamities. With all of us running around hepped up on adrenaline, no one was thinking clearly enough to do anything about the vampires we'd identified that were ready to suck victory from our project. In retrospect, we should have assigned someone to keep an eye on the big picture, mallet and wooden stake at the ready! In any given project things will certainly go wrong, so my approach is to plan for a few things going right in order to cancel those out.

LEARN FROM THE MOVIES: Sometimes when working on a particularly tough project I take to watching movies that have a high scrappiness factor. There's nothing better than a Bruce Willis "Die Hard" movie to bolster my courage when in the throes of a daunting project. Steven Seagal movies are another great source of courage and inspiration for those tasked to do the impossible. In one scene that I think perfectly depicts the nerve-jangling nature of some projects, Steven Seagal is running towards the back of a train that is in the midst of a head-on collision with another train. As he jumps from one collapsing car to the next, his buddy keeps a helicopter positioned so that a rope ladder dangles just outside of the back door of the caboose. Just as the train plunges into oblivion, Steven makes the leap to the dangling ladder. Wow! That scene has seen me through more nail-biter projects than you can imagine. Just make sure that you have someone you trust in the helicopter, otherwise you and your project could plunge right into an abyss.

The Biggest Fear. Most truly breakthrough projects have a fair degree of risk associated with them. That's for a good reason—they haven't been done before, so success is not assured. Remember the #1 reason that teams fail? Lack of clear goals! So of course if you are determined to lead your team to a successful finish on a breakthrough project you'll need clear goals, but it's not as easy as you think. The #1 reason most people resist setting goals, particularly challenging goals, is fear of failure.

From the US to Eastern Europe to Japan, I have found that fear of failure dwarfs the dreams, hopes, and aspirations of Earthlings around the world and at all levels in the organization. This ubiquitous fear causes individuals to take refuge in incremental thinking and the safety of nebulous, ill-defined commitments to which they can't possibly be held accountable. The result? Weasel words in specs, ambiguous commitment dates in action items, and incremental project goals.

It seems to me that the proportion of high tech product development projects that are truly innovative, compared to those that are incremental extensions of past projects, has shrunk dramatically in the past decade. Instead of Rev. 2.0 we get 1.1, 1.2, and 1.2.1. If you can't tolerate the possibility of failure you must be extremely careful what you start. In fact, many large companies have abandoned innovation entirely, choosing to acquire innovation rather than attempt to produce it from within. This is a perfectly sane choice. If you innovate you're bound to fail from time to time. Big companies can't risk it. Smaller, scrappier companies have a significant mental advantage.

The Innovating David vs. the Incremental Goliath? Consider a project team in a start-up company with no established reputation, nothing to lose but a few years and a couple of million bucks, and a fierce determination to risk everything to win. This team is in a much better position to innovate than is a project team in a large company. Adrift on a sea of budget cuts, schedule crunches, and lukewarm executive sponsors determined not to be left holding the bag on a failed project, large companies can sometimes retreat into playing it safe. This is indeed the grand illusion. There's no safety in the comfort zone. Most successful big companies that were around 100 years ago don't exist today.

But who can blame these risk-averse execs? Who in their right mind wants to champion upgrading the robustness of a software platform when it won't deliver new functionality that's obvious to the customer? Sales won't be clamoring for that as the top priority. It's just not that sexy to be the advocate for a good, solid foundation for the next ten years of products.

Let's make it personal. Suppose you were going to put $100K into fixing up your house. Which would you enjoy more: reinforcing the foundation, or remodeling your bathrooms with Italian marble and slate and putting in a brand new, state-of-the-art kitchen? On the surface, it is far more gratifying to keep extending the current platform until it crashes and burns—hopefully on the next guy's watch.

In larger companies with dozens of projects, the potential downside for taking on high-risk projects is way out of proportion to the upside. Success is quickly forgotten, while any failure lives on interminably in the memories of coworkers like some neural zombie. One of my colleagues, who works in a very large company, has borne the stench of one failed project wafting after him in the hallway for almost a decade. This failure has reduced his chances at other leadership jobs there, and he is finally seriously considering going elsewhere instead of waiting for all of the people who remember that unfortunate incident to either retire or die. Funnily enough, many people agreed that this project was huge, unwieldy, and ill-conceived from the start, but this guy was the project manager so he took the fall for it, and he's still paying a price.

It takes real commitment to the long-term greater good to build the foundation for future success. Unfortunately, most companies don't reward people for contributing to long-term results; they reward them for achieving their own annual performance goals, or even worse, focus exclusively on monthly or quarterly numbers. In such an environment, why should anyone take on the role of championing a product in an emerging technology with a risky market future? Better draft the feature list for revision 1.1.7.

Look Risk in the Eye. It you ask me, risk should be the motivating factor for taking on a new project, not the fear factor. Where there's risk there's the possibility of success, the kind that your company may not have seen before. This kind of success brings with it a recognition that you'd never obtain by doing just another incremental project. If you happen to fail, ouch! That'll leave a mark, but you'll live. You can only fail if you dare greatly. Besides, people generally over-estimate their risk of failure, mostly because at the beginning of a long journey it's difficult to imagine how every twist and turn will unfold.

I remember the sick feeling in the pit of my stomach during the early phases of my first few projects. Nothing was certain except that the chunk of work ahead was huge and the path to victory shrouded in mystery. However, little by little the veils were lifted, and the journey unfolded more or less favorably. Sometimes there were unsavory stretches, and frequently there were a whole lot of tasks that I didn't relish, to say the least. During such moments I've always followed the proverb, "When you have three big, ugly frogs to swallow, start with the biggest and ugliest one first." (Burp!)

Risk and failures can be stepping-stones to success. Just don't hang those stones around your neck; keep them underfoot instead, helping you identify and avoid the same mistakes in the future. When you do fail, don't carry the baggage of one failed project on to the next. One man's failure is another man's character-building experience. Wrap an interpretation around the experience that won't leave you seeking mental-health counseling for the next decade. (It doesn't help, anyhow.) Learn from the experience. Sink into the icy couch of despair for a while, wallow in your self-pity, then acknowledge the failure and move on. And don't start playing it safe! The safety of the comfort zone is complete illusion for those with a long-term perspective. Sometimes you'll get skewered for failure, or your career may suffer. Oh well, you were looking for work when you found that job, right?!! Get busy networking with all of the people who admire and respect you and get the hell out of there!

Give Choice a Voice. Trust your team. Even if you can't imagine how to snatch victory from the salivating jaws of defeat, they will probably figure out a way. I have found that each team member has dozens of great ideas for reducing risks and increasing the chances of success on any project. Without the instigation of the project manager, most of these ideas will never see the light of day. Team members can suffer tunnel vision as they focus on surviving the next week's deadlines. Even if they know of ways that could dramatically improve the chances of success, most people I've encountered won't voice them. They assume that their ideas won't be appreciated, or their requests won't be granted, and so they remain locked into an entirely predictable pattern of minimizing failure rather than maximizing success.

Feel the power! ... of your team, that is. Unleash them to consider possible ways to reduce the risk, accelerate the project, pull in the schedule, reduce the cost, and increase the performance, quality, and overall success of the project. Now *that's* your secret weapon, a pre-emptive strike against disaster!

7 Priority? Everything Is #1!

Prioritize ruthlessly, choosing between heart, lungs & kidneys if necessary.

"Never mistake motion for action." – Ernest Hemingway

One thing is for sure, there is always more to do on any project than there is time or money to do it all. And as much as people hate to choose between things that seem equally vital, if everything is top priority, nothing is. In the past, project teams used to ask for a list of "musts" and "wants" of the features required in a product. Now *everything* is a must. The triple constraint of schedule, cost, and features used to mean that the team would optimize one and constrain another while letting the third float. Now teams are expected to deliver good, fast, and cheap all at once, and pull off myriad miracles along the way.

Goal Seems a Little Hazy? Wear Your "Priorities" Spectacles. Many executives refuse to prioritize the "critical few" out of the "important many." When they tell me "They're all #1," I lean back, smile broadly, picture a farm and say aloud, "Ah, smell that dairy air!" They usually get the point.

The real tragedy of the failure to prioritize is the missed opportunity to leverage the judgment of each team member in the gazillions of decisions that they'll make during the project. When executives and other project stakeholders refuse to prioritize quality, features, schedule, cost, and other vital success criteria, people make up their own. Without guidance on the relative priority of project goals, each individual will be making decisions based on their own assumptions and beliefs about the priorities.

No one wants to choose between their heart, their lungs, and their kidneys. But when push comes to shove, the heart is #1 because you die within a minute, lungs are #2 because you can live three minutes without them, and kidneys are #3 because you can go on dialysis. While this sounds somewhat harsh, I've never met anyone who would choose their kidneys over their heart in a pinch. Of course, if the success criteria aren't clear, then putting those criteria in priority order won't be an easy matter, so you have to start by knowing what results you intend to achieve. Many teams aren't even clear about that, so it's no wonder they can't make tough choices among competing priorities.

The Why of Prioritization. Setting priorities is one of the most clarifying things that a leader can do for an organization. You may find, as one of my clients did, that managers have little to do once they are not constantly reassigning resources, moving people from one project to the next like some human electron-hole theory simulation to address what appears to be a constantly shifting urgent focus, and sorting out disagreements over which fire to fight next.

There are huge productivity hits associated with excessive multi-tasking, which can cause productivity losses as high as 60%. Working on seven to ten projects at once may seem an attractive way to get more done, but this is more of an illusion of progress than actual progress. A typical engineer who is forced to work on more than three different projects at a time ends up being less than 40% productive. This means that they now have to work ten hours to get four hours of work done. Being committed to success, of course, they work overtime (80 hours a week instead of the usual 60 to 70) to make up for this. They end up falling further behind, as putting in even more hours tends to further reduce productivity. Sure, they feel busy, but now they're working ten hours to get three hours of work done.[9]

Here's a list of reasons why you should insist on having priority lists and what you should do if you want them to be effective:

- They MUST be used when facing a crunch and either/or decisions need to be made. "We can either do priority #2 or #3." The choice is very clear and can be made at the worker level, without the delay of seeking guidance from the over-worked manager.

- They MUST drive behavior and choices.

- They MUST be reviewed, reset, and communicated periodically, so they are not perceived to be out of date.

- They MUST be easily accessible to everyone who is impacted by the work—ideally on an intranet site, or better yet, as the screen saver on everyone's computer.

- They are NOT intended to give people a reason to work only on the #1 priority. Not every resource allocation decision is an either/or. Usually we should be saying, "We can work on #1 and #2 and #3."

Prioritization isn't something we do to create a list of things we won't do. It forces us to clarify what's important in a project so we can focus our limited resources where they matter most.

Your project may require more than one priority list. Set priorities within your project among all critical success criteria. Set priorities among different projects that are sharing the same resources. Set priorities for setting priorities! Don't settle for spineless shoe shuffling and, "They're all #1." Your team deserves better, and they will perform better when you give them clear guidance on this.

---

9. Preston G. Smith and Don Reinertsen, *Developing Products in Half the Time: New Rules, New Tools, 2nd Edition* (New York: John Wiley & Sons, 1997), p. 207.

The People Perspective on Priorities. The executive sponsor is the most important person on your team. If you don't have one, STOP READING RIGHT NOW AND GO GET ONE! The project sponsor is your protection from the vicissitudes of the executive team, and your connection to the business goals of your organization. Without one you are vulnerable, and liable to deliver a project that isn't aligned with the business goals even if it is successful. At best, your team may be underappreciated. At worst, you risk career suicide without the guidance and support of someone with major weight at the executive level. This is the person at which the priority-setting buck stops.

So, how do you get your sponsor and the execs to make those tough choices? Ask, cajole, explain, plead, beg, insist, demand that priorities be clarified. If all else fails, grow a backbone and set them yourself. Publicize them widely. They'll let you know if you've set them incorrectly. Insist on clear priorities while you shovel against the tide!

Typically, a priority list should have a resource allocation table alongside, so that it acts as a resource allocation tool for the project managers. Graphic 7 is an example of one such priority list for four projects that are sharing the same resources: K, M, D and J. (Sorry, my brain froze up and I couldn't think of more clever names. Bartender, more tequila!)

Graphic 7: Priority List for Sharing Resources Across Several Projects

Priority List

Project	Resource Assignments
#1 – Heart	K K M M D
#2 – Lungs	K J M D
#3 – Kidneys	J J
#4 – Other Organs	D

SCRAPPY TIP: *Give your team three minutes to prioritize the parts of a car from the list below. For big groups, have them break into smaller teams of four to six people, and then compare results.*

Transmission	Engine	Ignition
Cooling System	Driver's Seat	Brakes
Gas Pedal	Steering Wheel	Heater
Air Conditioner	Passenger's Seat	Wheels and Tires
Lights	GPS System	Rearview Mirror

While there is no right or wrong answer, it's interesting to observe how teams attack this task. Usually people will begin this exercise randomly sorting the items, without much conscious thought about the criteria they are using to prioritize them. As they continue, they begin to understand that they need more information about the goals for the car, what it will be used for, the terrain it will be driven on, time of day, environmental conditions, and what matters most to the customer.

Why don't people set priorities? I think it's because they don't understand how to use them properly and fear they will result in critical work being put on the back-burner forever. Not so. A priority list actually increases the amount of work that gets done, as much as doubling productivity, by reducing the waste caused by constantly jumping from task to task like a Chihuahua that ate a pile of espresso beans.

After a while, setting priorities can become positively addictive! Once you get the hang of prioritizing, you may find yourself rank-ordering everything from chores to TV shows to former lovers. It's very clarifying to realize that the household task that you're working on is #13 on your list and you're only doing it to avoid the #1 most important thing you should be doing, like filing your tax returns or completing your on-line traffic school. When you don't have the luxury of limitless time or money, priorities will set you free.

8 Change? What Do You Mean Things Have Changed?

Anticipate and accommodate necessary and inevitable change.

"It is not the strongest of the species that survives, or the most intelligent, but the one most responsive to change." – Charles Darwin

When has any one of us worked on a project where nothing's changed? OK, time's up: NEVER! How's that old joke go? "Change is inevitable, except from vending machines." What I can't get through my overly thick skull is why project teams seem so surprised when change happens to them.

Come on, it's a miracle when the customer knows what they want in the first place, so when they change their mind, why should we lift our eyes toward heaven and ask, "Why me, God?" Team members have the nerve to get sick. How thoughtless of them! Schedules slip. (Now there's a surprise!) Execs promise full staffing from project kickoff, but people are still pretty busy cleaning up the debris from the last project, so it doesn't materialize. There's usually a very good reason—some previous catastrophe that still requires a bit of attention from the people assigned to your project—but it does impact your schedule. Well, duh!

Inescapable Change. If you've been managing projects for more than a week or two, very likely you've encountered changes to your project. Change is bound to happen. It's as inevitable as the weather and taxes. We can play the BMW card (bitch, moan, and whine) but it's sure as sunrise. While I'm pretty suspicious of pundits who start off with, "There are three primary causes of blah, blah, blah," here I go anyhow.

There are three kinds of change in projects:

- INEVITABLE: It was pretty much a sure thing from the start. Only wishful thinking prevented us from including it in the original project plans.

- UNFORTUNATE: We glimpsed it out of the corner of our eye, kept fingers and toes crossed, and kept our lucky charm handy, but—DANG!—it happened anyway.

- COMPLETE SURPRISE: Whoa! Totally blindsided us! Only the clairvoyant could have seen it coming. (Note: This hardly ever happens in projects, but I include it for completeness.)

In other words, most of the changes that will insinuate themselves into a project are predictable. So let's not have all kinds of weeping, wailing, and gnashing of teeth when it happens. Deal with it! Only the clueless persist in the belief that a project can be conceived, defined, planned, executed, and completed without changes. That's a big force behind Agile and other popular methodologies (most of which have been around for years, but now have been applied to software and have much snappier names than when we invented them in hardware manufacturing decades ago). The world, the stage upon which we strut and fret, is a rapidly changing one. Scrappy Project Managers simply must accommodate change in their project planning and execution. My wardrobe is out of style before I hang my latest dress in my closet, and computer technology is obsolete by the time I drive to the office and boot up my PC, so why should I expect a project to be any different?

Don't Fan the Flames of Change. As heartily as I asserted that change is unavoidable, I advise you not to feed the fire. Unless you're rapidly approaching senility, a total amnesiac, or completely new to project management, you can pretty well guess some of the things that are going to change in your project:

- Customers will change their minds.

- Resources will be re-directed elsewhere.

- Markets will shift, or collapse entirely.

- Team members will get sick, take vacation, or quit, possibly all three.

- Priorities will change, and change back, and change again.

- Alliance partners will re-organize.

- Budgets will be cut, and then cut again.

- Suppliers won't ship parts on time.

- Critically needed parts won't meet spec.

- Products will have unexpected errors discovered late in the test cycle.

- Schedules will slip. And slip again. And again.

In the interest of brevity, I've left off the other 317 things that typically change on a project. Besides, I don't want to take all of the fun out of this for you by giving you too much information up front. The bottom line is that, like so many aspects of project management, change is mandatory and liking it is optional. Get busy adapting to and implementing change, rather than struggling against its Sisyphean nature. Reduce the likelihood of change by anticipating it. Build it into your project plans from day one, and accept the fact that it's going to be your constant companion.

Self-inflicted Wounds. As satisfying as it would be to pin the change donkey's tail onto some other person's butt, sometimes we're the culprits. Did the customer really need that extra feature that we added? Did the User Guide have to be on par with the *Iliad* and the *Odyssey*? Did we honestly need to review each and every bug in the cumulative database that's been tracked since time immemorial? Sometimes "good enough" is. Super-geeks will want to make sure that the space shuttle can be launched from the user interface, but the product's ultimate market success rarely rests upon these feature creeps or feature leaps.

In one late-phase situation, a well-intentioned VP of Engineering wandered into a developer's office inquiring, "What would it take to add blah, blah, blah...?" (You can fill in the blah, blahs. I'm sure you've heard it all!) This developer was more than happy to drop what they were doing and stuff yet another toy into the already feature-rich UI. When I discovered it, I snarled through clenched teeth, "Take it out!" "But it's already done, Kimberly!" Ha! The coding is just the beginning. What about testing and documenting it? Take it out, we did.

He hadn't given a moment's thought to the implications of such late changes to the goals of our project: high quality and an on-time schedule. Every hour of software development racks up about two hours of possible testing, and we just didn't have the bandwidth to assure that it would operate properly in the final product without causing unforeseen ripple-effect bugs. A big, whopping share of bugs in shipped products results from changes like this. Small changes are even worse than big ones because people underestimate the threat they pose to product quality, and so tend to under-test them.

Change Kills! Did I mention that people generally loathe change? Don't believe anything I say just because I act like I know what I'm talking about—that's just a bad habit I picked up in graduate school. Prove it to yourself. Try wearing your watch on the other arm for a whole day. What starts out as an enlivening experience quickly turns into a source of irritation as you repeatedly glance at your bare arm, the one where that darned watch should be. Shifting where your watch is located isn't likely to cause irreparable damage, but I do recall one re-organization where a fellow walked out of the building after the announcement of some corporate downsizing ... rightsizing ...

capsizing (whatever they call it these days), and dropped dead in the parking lot from a heart attack. Never underestimate the potential impact of change on your team!

Hugging the Hydra of Change. Since you know change is coming, prepare for it. You don't need to bake it a cake, wave banners, and cheer about it, but change will be coming to the project party. Get your ducks lined up! No amount of hand-wringing or consternation will make your competitors revert to a previous version of their product. Wishful thinking will not eradicate the impact of some thoughtless team member who chooses to get married at the height of their involvement in the critical path. Exhortations and nebulous descriptions of impending doom will not dissuade a determined product manager from adding just one more feature to an already over-burdened "musts" list. Do the dexterity dance and ask, "What would make this possible?" Or, more specifically, "What does this apparently ill-conceived change in plans make possible that wouldn't have been possible had we run a sensible and viable project?" See? I'm sure you are feeling better already! I've found that a Bombay gin martini—straight up, three olives—is a terrific catalyst for thinking outside of the bun during times of involuntary change. Ask for the neon pink swizzle stick with the little flamingo ornament on it for an extra giggle while you soothe your frazzled nerves.

Let's Play with Gumby Again! Today's projects demand not just a tolerance for change, but an enthusiastic embrace of it. The change-savvy project manager knows that a schedule isn't worth the paper it's printed on, that the requirements are a rough approximation, and the initial goals are little more than a mass hallucination. From the moment the starting shot is fired, the change game is afoot. Assurances of resource commitments melt in the hard light of day. Gantt charts and PERT charts distort into unrecognizable semblances of their former selves. Handshake deals for budget and all manner of support take on a disturbing palsy. Get used to it.

While it would be cathartic to vilify the culprits, they're well-intentioned chaps just like us, who are squeezed between the unlikely and the impossible. Don't be Pokey. Scrappy Project Managers are like our old friend Gumby, flexible as a gymnast! Plan for, and figure out a way to accommodate, change. Start from the first nanosecond of your project. It's coming as sure as the 3 AM infomercial.

Managing change is like going bear hunting with a whip. Here are a few guidelines that will keep you from being mauled:

- **Eyes Wide Open:** Don't let Mr. Change be the surprise guest at your project party. Since change has absolutely and positively RSVP'd to your project, do make a list of the highest-impact changes that you and your team anticipate, and then create a plan for dealing with them lickety-split.

- **Keep Track:** Track the changes that occur on your project. Even a short project is likely to be transformed by dozens of shape-shifting metamorphoses. Keep a list. You'll be using it at the post mortem, or to explain to those who caused the changes why other, more important, goals of the project weren't met. And it's amusing to read, too. "Entire company IT system down for two days during super-important design phase requiring electronic file transfer of critical path design." Ah, yes, someday we'll look back on this and laugh, then hurriedly change the subject.

- **Estimate the Impact:** Quantify the impact of changes to project goals. Eating a single chip doesn't wreck a diet. Eating a whole bag of those greasy snacks can set you back two months. Every time a key person gets pulled off development to support a trade show demo, catalog it. When features are added without adding staff or extending the schedule, capture the impact it will have. Not only will it give you something to do during the 10 to 20 nanoseconds you're not busy with other project management tasks, you'll decrease the mystery surrounding why all manner of project goals aren't met. This chronology will also prove pretty handy when you get asked, "What's taking so long?"

- **Change is Opportunity Disguised as Dog Poo.** Scrappy Project Managers are nothing if not opportunists. When the fickle finger of fate points in your direction, look for the possibility hidden in the project mutation. Is there a poorly-supported feature that needs to be added, a test that needs to be run, a design review that needs to be held, that can be inserted in the midst of the other change? Activities that otherwise might have extended the critical path might now nestle inconspicuously under the wings of changes with more enthusiastic support. Keep a list of such "wish we had time to" ideas, wait for your chance, and then pounce! As a project leader you should never be the cause of delay, but you can judiciously plan to be the beneficiary of delays forced upon you.

Impossible Changes. Sometimes, teams are asked to make what seems like an impossible change. Don't be so quick to assume that something is impossible. Human brains generally assume that anything that they cannot immediately imagine is highly unlikely or unrealistic at best. Considering that most people have access to less than 1% of all wisdom and knowledge, I wouldn't be too quick to dismiss any possibility without at least reflecting on it for a spell.

Although they might seem like mal-intentioned project saboteurs, the people asking for the change usually have not thought about the implications of what they are asking. So my answer is always "Yes, if...." For example, I might rattle off the following in response to something that strikes me as a ridiculous request: "Sure, we can get this project out 4 months sooner if you cut 3 'musts' from the feature list, increase the budget by $175,000 and stop pulling our engineers off of this project to fix irritating bugs in the last version." Or, in more extreme cases, "Absolutely, we can ensure 99.99999999% uptime if we change the gravitational constant of the universe and run time backward. Einstein said we could! Let's get busy on this right away." Saying no doesn't cut it, but saying, "Yes, if the moon and the stars align and your good karma holds," is the mark of a can-do kind of guy.

Whatever your approach to change management, keep in mind that managing change is like managing a tornado. You can shout orders all you want, but the house will still be flying around in 150 mph winds and will likely end up on some character wearing striped socks and a pointed hat. Auntie Em! Toto! Get the hogs in the basement!

Note to Self: Check wardrobe and dispose of all striped socks and pointed hats!

9 Assumption Is A Mother

Challenge assumptions & beliefs, especially insidious self-imposed limitations.

"If we did it my way, we wouldn't be arguing."
– Napoleon

Assumption is the mother of most disasters. Consider what happens in projects when teams fail to challenge assumptions. There are loads of assumptions lurking about in your team's heads, such as, "The customer requirements are well understood" or "Goals are clear." We've all heard the clever joke, "When you ASSUME, you make an ASS out of U and ME." Scrappy Project Managers assume nothing.

Not Enough Time or Money. When I ask project team members about the biggest challenges they face, they usually say something like, "I don't have enough time to do everything that needs to be done," or, "There's not enough money in the budget to do the job right." Wow, what a surprise! Not enough time or money? Gosh, this certainly is an unusual project. Not!

Here's the real kicker: The next question I ask these folks is, "When you asked your manager/sponsor/executive for additional time or money, what did they say?" The typical response is extremely predictable. I'm sure you can guess the reply: "I didn't ask." Most people don't even bother to ask for what they need. They just assume that the request will be denied.

Here's the catch: requests are usually denied the first time they are made. When people go to "We Be Executives" training they are taught to say no when asked for resources of any kind. "No" is the answer that any manager worth their salt is supposed to give to at least the first and second requests, particularly when the request is a panicked plea for help, with little or no supporting evidence, thought, or justification. Faced with much clamoring for more of every imaginable resource, managers grow fond of saying no repeatedly. Nevertheless, if you ask one time more than they refuse, you win! Sure, sometimes they might fire your ass for being such an unstoppable bastard before you get what you want, but if you really needed it to be successful, who cares? You were doomed anyhow.

Do Your Homework. But seriously, I've seen too many project leaders barge into an executive's office demanding more time, money, or people, with nothing more than a "Because I say so" justification uttering from their ill-prepared lips. Who can fault a busy project leader for not taking the time to build a stronger case? On the other hand, who can fault the executive for denying the request? It's a moot point, however, if people don't even bother to ask, prisoners in a snare of their own making. This is an example of learned helplessness. As in some well-known psychology studies on this topic, the jailer can walk away and leave the keys in the lock, and the prisoner will stay firmly inside their self-imposed cage.

Based on my own experience, Scrappy Project Managers pretty much always get what they ask for: additional people hired during a hiring freeze, additional money when there's no budget, equipment when there's none available, and all other manner of miracles. It's not magic.

If you don't ask, you don't get. Here are some common-sense principles to increase your chances of having your wishes granted by the executive genie:

- **Understand the goals of the person you are asking for help.** Everybody has something that they're trying to get done or that they're worried about. Even if they don't want to help you, there is a pretty good chance that they want to help themselves. If you can show them how helping you can help their sorry asses out of a bind, they will be much more enthusiastic about supporting your request.

- **Prepare before you make the request.** Bear in mind that preparation consists of more than muttering, "I'm going to give them a piece of my mind," as you storm down the hallway toward their office. Calm yourself with a few deep breaths. If necessary, breathe into a paper bag until your heart rate is at least below 150.

- **Make a clear and solid business case for your request.** This usually requires more than saying, "Trust me, I'm the project manager, and I need it because I say so."

- **Ask them what would make it possible for your request to be granted.** Sometimes they may not even be the right person to ask. Excuse me for stating the obvious, but if you are asking someone for something and they don't have the authority to grant it, then it's no big surprise when they don't give it to you. Executives aren't omnipotent. They are mere mortals like the rest of us, and their powers are finite. Identify the right person to grant your request, seek an audience, and beseech them like Dorothy in the *Wizard of Oz*. Carry a broom if you must; whatever works.

- **Even the Mighty have Limitations.** Project leaders have to dodge a lot of bullets in order to survive, thrive, and ultimately succeed. But our projects don't have to die of self-inflicted wounds. After years of researching the subject, I have found that executives and other managers do not crawl out of bed determined to bring a project to its knees—it just happens!

Executives frequently feel that they don't have enough time or money to do all that they are required to do. They have people riding them like rented mules just like we do. They are sometimes stressed out, confused, and frustrated. Their hands are often tied by business constraints that they aren't at liberty to discuss. Although I'm sure they'd like to confide in their project leaders, they can't very well reveal things that could devastate the morale of the team. "Gosh, I'd love to give you that extra money, but we only have three more months of operating funds in the bank. If we can't raise the next round of funding, we'll have to lay off you and your whole team." This just isn't a topic fit for open discussion. Or they may be dealing with a gaggle of cackling Wall Street analysts bemoaning earnings per share a quarter-cent lower than predicted. Or there may be half a dozen projects of higher priority with more urgent needs, which they are supporting whole-heartedly (in which case you would have benefited by ascertaining the priority of your project relative to others prior to making your request).

I can assure you of this: No executive ever let their own rules stop them from doing what was in their own best interest. As project leaders we don't rank highly enough not to ask for what we need. It's our responsibility to make it easy for others to see the right decision, and to build a strong case for granting our request that aligns with the company goals. It's the responsibility of the manager / sponsor / executive to consider whether to grant that request.

Never let the possibility of rejection curtail your requests. A boat adrift feels no resistance. It's only when we are moving in the direction of our goals that we start to feel the water dragging against our hulls. Resistance is a sign that we are moving. If you aren't feeling some, you're not pushing hard enough.

Headed for the Bermuda Triangle. I remember one time in particular when challenging assumptions about what was possible really paid off. We were a small-time company developing a piece of hardware that a Fortune 500 company was going to put their name on and stake their brand reputation to. We were caught in the surf of an impossible schedule, heading for the Bermuda Triangle of project death. We gathered the team together in the cargo hold of our ill-fated vessel (OK, it was a conference room, but it was rather humid) and provoked them into brainstorming possibilities that could get us out of the mess.

At first, most of the team members rolled their eyes and looked pityingly upon the doomed captain of this lost ship. (That would be me.) Then came the challenge that galvanized them into fighting mode. I gave them a stirring speech along these lines: "You may be right. This may be impossible. But humor me for ten minutes while we brainstorm at least one idea that would be guaranteed to fail, and one idea that would get us all fired." They rather fancied this challenge, and a hailstorm of ridiculous proposals issued from the ranks.

As our creativity was loosed, these were followed by somewhat plausible suggestions, and finally a recommendation that was a veritable "Jaws of Life" for this project. We would ask the customer to let us ship the final hardware product with beta-version software, which would be automatically updated upon first customer use. This would save us at least a month over the best schedule we could muster. We waltzed triumphantly to the office of our project sponsor, who immediately shot it down. He assured us that he'd already thought of it, asked our customer, and that the idea had been rejected.

But being that we were seriously scrappy, we didn't take no for an answer. Undaunted, we begged, "Can we at least ask again?" You see, we had a scheme that involved more than simply putting the request to them. We sent our most likeable engineer to visit our customers in person, armed with a credit card and a big, lovable smile. He had specific instructions to curry favor with them through any legal means possible—including those involving a risk of shame, disgrace, and personal ruin (karaoke)—indulging them in all manner of spirits and mischief. Then, and only then, was he to steer our partners back to the test lab and have a look at our prototypes.

Since our goal was to demonstrate how easy it would be for customers to update the software on production units, we had conveniently loaded an obsolete version of the software on the prototypes prior to his trip. "No problem!" he proclaimed, and spritely downloaded the latest software from across the planet before their very eyes. When they saw how easy it was, they agreed to allow us to ship with non-final software, shaving a month off what would otherwise have been an "impossible" schedule. And this was only one of several hefty assumptions that we challenged along the way.

Thinking Out of the Box. On another project, it was clear that we'd have to be extremely lucky to hit an aggressive release date for a product that had a market window narrower than a slit in a Venetian blind. Since this team had been around the block a time or two, we were all pretty sure that at least one or two bugs would be discovered late in the process that would put the kibosh on shipping this product on time. We didn't know which bugs, of course, or we wouldn't have created the darn things in the first place. So we decided to ask for a big chunk of cash to build dozens of additional prototypes months before the hardware design was complete, and well before the software was even close to final. We shipped these barely-functioning protos to surrogate customers all over the country with a simple request: Beat the tar out of them and find problems early, while we finish the design. We also shipped off a few of the extremely precious remaining units to the HALT test chamber (Highly Accelerated Life Testing) where they were simultaneously heated, shaken, and stirred into a frenzy of purposely-induced product failure.

HALT is a tough test to build support for among certain analytical types because it puts the product through way more rigorous conditions than the customer ever will, or even than in the specs. But I wouldn't consider developing a hardware product where quality matters without it, since it reveals points of design weakness that will never surface during in-spec types of testing. Sure, sometimes you'll find some failure modes that would never have been a problem in the field, and sometimes you will miss things that aren't accelerated by earth, wind, and fire approaches. But in this case, these early tests revealed two defects that, had they been discovered just prior to launch, would have stopped shipment for at least a month while the design was changed and tested. If they had been discovered after products got into the hands of customers they could have resulted in a complete recall of the product. Whew, that was close! Now, can you guess what the execs had said when we first suggested these drastic risk-reducing measures? "No!" See what I mean? Ultimately, we were both glad that we didn't let that stop us.

Play Your Part. Of course, there are a few completely boorish and unreasonable tyrants roaming loose out in the world who rule by force and intimidation. I've crossed paths with people who are completely unresponsive to even the most well-prepared and substantiated request. They are rare, and when I realize I'm working with such a so-called human being I usually flee the room. Never wrestle with a pig! You get dirty, and the pig likes it. Some businesses deserve to fail.

Even rational execs lose their minds and make a bad call now and then. Why? Who knows?! The air gets pretty thin up there in the executive ranks. The important thing is to separate the request-making from the request-granting process. Request-making must continue in step with the needs. Request-granting is frequently someone else's purview, and you mustn't let their inability to fulfill your needs interfere with your ability to ask for what you need.

When all's said and done, though, we wouldn't be very scrappy as project leaders if we just blamed others or cast ourselves upon the generosity of some passing executive. In some cases, team members themselves squarely block the path to project success. Many things can hinder progress. Sometimes it's doing things the same old way, refusing to consider alternatives that seem unpleasant or difficult, or being blind to our own power to make a difference to the project's success. I always find it more effective to look in the mirror first before looking around to find out who's holding me back. It's usually me.

Pre-emptive Pessimism. The most widespread assumption that plagues the world of projects is the one that I call "Pre-emptive Pessimism," the immediate assumption that something is impossible. This may be observed in an executive sponsor, a member of your project team, suppliers, alliance partners, people working on other projects which are competing for resources with you, or even from yourself. When your executive sponsor is wallowing in pessimism, it's a real test of your abilities as a project leader. You'll need to protect your team from this negative influence and single-handedly inspire them to exceed these negative expectations.

There are a variety of causes underlying the tendency to assume that something is impossible when it's just very difficult. Some are innocent, and some nefarious. It can be very convenient to assume that something is impossible. For one thing, this removes the need to even attempt to accomplish the task. Declaring that something is impossible reduces expectations, workloads, and the risk of failure. And sometimes people just don't want to do it, or have some other political axe to grind.

Most of the time I think it's just a matter of people assuming that something that they can't immediately figure out how to do *must* be impossible. As human beings, the less we know, the more confident we become, so I never let these people stop me from at least making a valiant attempt. If someone says something is impossible, a Scrappy Project Manager will generally set about to prove it by exhausting all possible means of making it happen.

Don't get me wrong. I'm a big fan of negative thinking and I highly recommend holding a "negative thinking session" occasionally to blow off steam and have a good laugh. Negativity is quite handy in risk identification and mitigation, as we've seen. And a healthy dose of negativity can be an extremely practical self-protective mechanism that prevents us from blurting out "I'll do it!" when asked to take the helm of a project tilting toward tragedy. But we're all prone to over-estimating the complexity of a task at the start, and underestimating our capabilities. So when someone says something is impossible, get busy on it! Chances are you won't have much competition for the task.

No matter who is the source, pessimism often stems from low self-confidence. If your team has a pessimistic member, embrace their negativity as a valuable component of the diverse perspectives on the team. Then guide, or goad, them into exceeding their own dismal predictions of what's possible. Believe me, even the most uncooperative team member will eventually be grateful if you get them to out-perform their own expectations of themselves. This will do wonders for their self-confidence, and you will get better performance from them on subsequent projects. One word of caution. Like the appreciation of children for their parents, it may take 30 or so years to manifest, so don't expect people to immediately shower you with praise for proving that the biggest obstacle to their success was their own self-limiting beliefs. It might take a while to come back to you.

Challenge Assumptions. No one can give you what you deny yourself. Take a course on "How to Get Out of Your Own Way" and overcome the obstacles of your own making first. Then you will be free to move on to other, more complicated challenges standing in the way of your team's success. Take a hint from the Queen of Hearts in *Alice in Wonderland*, and every day make a list of the top six things that seem impossible, but if they were possible, would transform your project for the better. Then go ask for help to make these things happen! One thing's for sure, if you don't ask, you don't get.

10 So, What Were You Expecting?

Manage the expectations of all stakeholders: under-promise & over-deliver.

"You cannot build a reputation on what you are going to do." – Henry Ford

One sure path to project doom is failure to manage the expectations of the many people who will judge your project's success. Myriad stakeholders have a keen interest in the outcome of your project. Executives may be counting on revenues from new products for critical business results. Suppliers may be poised to make investments based on milestones and forecasts. With any luck, managers will plan their resources around your project requirements, and team members may plan their personal lives (if they have any) around your schedule. Ultimately, the customers will be the final judge of whether your project met not just their needs, but also their expectations.

As any experienced salesperson can tell you, the secret to a delighted customer is to under-promise and over-deliver. It's difficult enough to do with those you know are expecting something from your team. It's impossible if you don't even know they're expecting something! Assiduously avoid last-minute surprises involving previously unidentified stakeholders who pop up just in time to derail success. Your ability to identify all relevant stakeholders and their interests, and to effectively manage their expectations throughout the project, can have more to do with your ultimate success than the minutia of features, schedules, and sales figures.

Happiness is Relative. If Einstein were a psychologist, he would have studied the relativity of happiness as a result of the gap between expectations and reality. Stress and disappointment in life have more to do with this gap than with what actually happens. All sorts of interesting experiments have demonstrated this—mostly with rats, but there are some similarities to humans, so bear with me.

Studies have shown that if rats receive a warning signal before they are shocked, they are less distressed by the shock.[10] Similarly, humans seem to be able to deal with the stress of project life much better if they have some idea of what is coming at them. And if you teach rats to avoid shock by pressing a lever, they will persist in pressing that lever even when it doesn't do any good. The little rascals won't give up! In fact, the experimenters shocking the poor little rodents gave up first. This phenomenon is known as "learned mastery," and is quite the opposite of the equally fascinating "learned helplessness" that shows up in rats, humans, and other mammals.[11]

I'm not suggesting that we can learn a lot about working with other people by studying rats, although as I write this I am beginning to see enough similarities to make me uncomfortable. But our expectations certainly do influence the perception of our experiences. Stress or happiness has more to do with the difference between what we were expecting and what we got than the misery index of the experience itself. The gap between expectations and reality is also what determines how delighted or disappointed people are with the results of a project. That's why it's so important that project managers actively

---

10. *Science*, August 31, 1962, Vol. 137, No. 3531, pp. 665-666.
11. Learned Helplessness Research, University of Pennsylvania's Positive Psychology Center, http://www.ppc.sas.upenn.edu/lh.htm

set and manage expectations of all key stakeholders, from the start of a project right on through the "Thanks for doing such a great job!" love-fest celebration at the end.

Identifying Project Stakeholder Expectations. Human beings are constantly comparing what happens to what was expected. When I returned from a lengthy trip abroad I expected all of my houseplants to be dead due to lack of watering, because I asked my husband to water them while I was away. But he had installed an automatic watering system, so only the ones he forgot to connect to the drip system were dead. I was delighted beyond words. Likewise, the key to delighting your stakeholders is to deliver just a bit more than they expected, just a little earlier, with just a touch more quality. If you promise the stars and only deliver the moon you won't impress anyone.

There are plenty of ways to run afoul of expectations in any project. The most obvious is to fall short of expectations for schedule, budget, features, and quality. These are the easiest to measure, but expectations may also exist around the frequency and tone of communication, the format of status reports, and other conventions or business practices.

An open dialogue at an in-person meeting with each stakeholder is a terrific way to start your expectation management campaign. Ask each person what they will be saying at the end of the project if you are wildly successful and how they will measure that success. (This is a good time to ask about the relative priority of critical success factors, by the way.) Inquire as to what they see as their role in the project, and what part they'd like to play as it evolves. Then communicate what your role is, what you need from them in order to deliver the results they want, and let them know how you will be keeping them in loop.

Every relationship between two human beings eventually hits a bump in the road, so acknowledge right up front that there will be misunderstandings. Agree right then and there on how those will be escalated and resolved. When I was repairing analytical instruments for HP I always offered new customers my manager's business card while saying, "My goal is to delight you with the service we offer. If there is ever a time when I'm not meeting your needs and you can't get through to me, please feel free to call my boss and discuss it with him and we'll work together to sort things out for you." They rarely called, and when they did it was annoying, to be sure. But I'd much rather have my boss riding my butt about something that's aggravating a customer than to have one seething silently in the wings.

In project teams, I've been known to pass out "Escalation Cards" to people involved with the project saying, "When (not if, but WHEN) there's a problem of any kind, or something doesn't meet your expectations, please call the following number and let's discuss it lickety-split." I put my contact info on the cards, along with my boss's contact info, in case the bee buzzing around in their bonnet is me.

Managing Customer Hallucinations. If you've done a fantastic job of exhaustively defining clear, unambiguous, and well-defined goals up front, to which your customer has unconditionally agreed, you may think your work is done. Not so! When it comes to customers, there is no requirement, specification, or agreement that cannot be misunderstood. That's why project success depends on continuing to manage customer expectations throughout the entire project.

Think the software requirements are clear as sunlight? Get the screenshots and "use cases" in front of the customer to make sure that they share your hallucination. Imagine that there's only one way to interpret the hardware design spec? Get a foam model of the gadget into the customer's hands, and find out what you missed. Do your engineers think the product is intuitively obvious, easy to use, and simple enough for a child to follow, that the user manual is superfluous, and that any twelve-year-old with half a brain could install the product without guidance? Run a "follow me home" experiment, where one of your team members silently observes a novice customer unpacking the product, setting it up, and learning to use it. For a whole bushel of fun, record a video of the experience and show it to any engineer who insists on classifying ease-of-use bugs as "enhancement requests."

There never seems to be enough time to include the voice of the customer during a hectic project. But if you don't keep your customers in the loop and seek their feedback at every step along the way, you might just as well add a couple of months to your schedule for the debate and rework that's going to be required, or cut a couple of million off of your revenue projections. Either way, it's generally faster and cheaper to avoid this pitfall than to end up spinning your wheels later in the sand trap of disappointment.

Mystery of the Missed Deadlines. When high-level executives are closely involved in project execution, the political landscape can be a bit more dicey. This became clear to me when I was consulting with a company that was struggling to launch a new product—a complicated mixture of hardware and embedded software—in a more predictable and reliable way than the fits and starts of their previous launches. The forlorn VP of Products lamented, "I have no idea when the product will ship, if at all!" The project managers in his organization didn't want to disappoint him, so when pressed, they waved their hands furiously about, did a little tap dance, muttered something incomprehensible about there being a lot of uncertainty associated with the project, and hastily beat a retreat from the project review meetings. "We're on the bleeding edge of science and discovery!" the engineers would claim. "You can't schedule this kind of innovation!"

How many times have we heard this claim that creativity can't be scheduled? I'm not so sure. When the king asked Mozart to write a musical piece within a week for a regal affair, I'll bet that Mozart got creative. As a matter of fact, imposing constraints on the creative process can channel the creativity rather than constraining it. Sure, some projects are truly dependent on a completely unpredictable discovery. But most of the time, the breakthrough required involves having enough imagination to estimate a squishy task accurately, not solving the mysteries of the universe.

Not put off by such tactics, our VP of Products persistently quizzed the project leaders on schedules, milestones, and delivery dates. These intrepid creatures responded with meticulously prepared Microsoft Project Gantt charts representing a schedule only slightly less whimsical than the final Harry Potter book. (This is a little off topic, and call me cynical, but I have to wonder if it is really the last Harry Potter Book, or some James Bond re-enactment of "Never Say Never," or maybe more along the lines of New Coke and Coke Classic.) Naturally these schedules weren't met. They were never met, but there were always plenty of "reasons" (a.k.a. excuses) for the project managers to escape blame. Determined to get to the bottom of this recurring strange behavior when I was called in to consult with this organization, I immediately put on my Sherlock Holmes outfit and started smoking a pipe. What on earth could explain smart, experienced, well-educated people falling into the same traps again and again?

It turns out that one of the reasons was a table-pounding guy on the executive team who would demand certain things happen by FM (friggin' magic), and who was extremely punitive toward those who failed to meet his unreasonable demands. As a result, those who had mortgages to pay, kids in college, or other reasons to value their careers avoided making any promises under any circumstances, and had plenty of butt-covering material handy in case they had to make a promise that they couldn't keep. Once this Neanderthal was removed from day-to-day contact with the project teams, the VP was able to have more open and honest dialogues with the project manager, get realistic commitments from the team, and hold the whole kit and caboodle of them to those commitments.

In Order to Manage Expectations You Must Set Expectations. By now I hope you're convinced that, in order to manage expectations, a project leader must be willing to set clear expectations in the first place. Nowhere is this more important than with the project sponsor. Sometimes the sponsor thinks that the extent of their sponsorship is providing funding. While I'm not overly into copiously documenting project details, it's vital that you clarify fundamental expectations, roles, and responsibilities on all sides in writing.

The best way I have found to set and manage expectations with the sponsor and others is to create a one-page project charter at the beginning of the project. Yes, I said all on one page! One page is about as much as you can count on people reading without you standing over them. Even better, put your entire high-level plan on a 3 x 5 post-it note, and stick it somewhere that you and your sponsor will see it all the time. With executives, less is more. They've got a few more things on their minds than your project, so don't expect them to read and thoughtfully consider everything you send their way.

A one-page charter only needs to capture in the broadest strokes the following aspects of your project:

- What it is

- What it ISN'T

- Definition of "success"

- How "success" will be measured

- Who will work on it

- Critical success factors

- Assumptions

- Major risks and mitigation plans

- Relative priority of schedule, scope, budget, quality, other factors

- Target audience

- Distribution channels

- Rough schedule of business-driven milestones

- Rough budget

- Anything else you think mustn't be left to chance

When a project starts, sit down with your sponsor for an hour or so, listen intently to their pipe dreams about what they want out of this project, and ask probing questions that will allow you to create this document after your conversation is over. Then whip up a charter and send it to them on email. Wait a couple of days and ask if they have read it. (In most cases, you can guess the answer.) Then go in to their office and read it with them in person to be sure that you are quite literally on the same page. Then get them to sign it. After all, we're all amnesiacs from time to time. It's not like you're going to read it back to them on the witness stand in a court of law. It's more of a symbolic act, but in my experience it does carry great weight.

WARNING SIGNS: If you can't fit the intent of the project on one page, it's probably too complicated. If your sponsors don't have time to read one page, don't bother doing the project. It's probably not that important. If they can't spare five minutes up front to assure that the goals for the project are clear, you are unlikely to get any better support later.

The other nice thing about having a one-page charter is that you can quickly get new team members up to speed on the big picture as people come and go during the project. It's way better than explaining over and over what the project is, is not, yadda, yadda, yadda. Just write the damn charter! If you want a Microsoft® Word template and example, email me at kimberly@wiefling.com and I'll send you an example that I use when I come up for air.

Managing the Expectations of the Team. While you're busy bebopping around, managing the expectations of all of the various stakeholders, don't forget about your own team. In order to be maximally productive, team members need to know who's driving the bus, where they're headed, and what kind of progress they're making along the way. While it might be tempting to focus only on the growing pile of tasks needed to get the job done, you've missed a huge opportunity if you don't manage the expectations of your own team. Let's demonstrate this via a pop quiz.

Which of the following teams do you think would be more productive?

1. Told that this was the long march they had heard about, the team got busy marching.
2. Told they would march 20 miles, after 14 the team was told they only had 4 more to go.
3. Told they would march 15 miles, after 14 the team was told they had 6 more to go.
4. Told they would march 20 miles, the team was given progress up-dates every mile.

If you guessed #4, you win the expectations management "My Momma Didn't Raise No Fool" award. The last group can be expected to be up to 60% more productive than the least productive group.[12] The least productive group was the one where no one had a clue where they were going, how far they had traveled, or how much terrain lay ahead. It's pretty easy to figure out why. If you're adrift, you might as well wait and see where the current carries you.

Creating Clarity Out of Chaos. Sometimes there will be a lot of uncertainty in the goals, direction, and actual status of a project. Regardless, if you want to get the most out of your team, you need to create at least the illusion of clarity. When all else fails, make something up that cuts through the fog of reality and presents an understandable facsimile. Give your team a map of where you are, where you're going to end up, and how far along you reckon you are. Think about the fund-raising thermometers used by organizations like The United Way which track donations during their annual fund drives (somewhat akin to that shown in Graphic 8). The top of the thermometer clearly shows the total money they intend to raise. The level of red rises with each dollar donated. The gap between the current level and the top of the thermometer makes it clear how much more money is needed. And anyone who looks at this knows immediately how to make a difference—crack open your wallet and donate money!

---

12. Albert Bandura, "Health Promotion by Social Cognitive Means," *Health Education & Behavior*, Vol. 31, No. 2, p. 143-164 (2004). http://heb.sagepub.com/cgi/content/abstract/31/2/143

Graphic 8: United Way Thermometer Visual Goal & Status Tracking

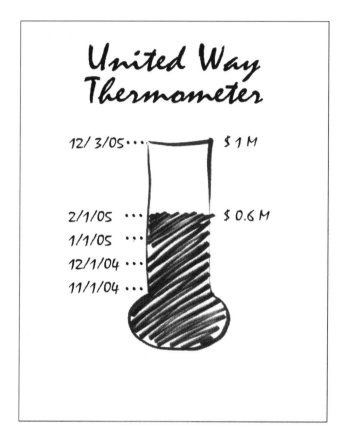

Make sure your team has an equally clear indicator of the route to success, something that indicates their status and progress versus the project goals in a compelling way that screams out, "Here's what needs doing next!" Like the United Way Thermometer, seeing their progress will inspire the team, and seeing the gap between where they are and where they need to be will encourage them to close that gap pronto.

Purposely Purposeless Customers. Sometimes customers benefit from keeping expectations fuzzy. If requirements aren't clear, they can keep you on the hook longer and nibble more from you in the end. Clear expectations protect you and your team. In one case, we assigned one of our team members the full-time task of clarifying customer expectation. This particular customer was intent on roasting us over the coals in a grueling i-dotting, t-crossing exercise before accepting the product. (Should it be a colon or a semi-colon?... Hmm... Better call a 3-hour meeting to discuss it.) Although it was an excruciating assignment, everyone was a lot happier when we had every single screenshot exactly as it would appear in the final product agreed to and signed off by the customer. By tackling this exercise before the product was ready to ship, we probably saved a couple of weeks of dealing with last-minute minutiae, including the back-and-forth review and approval process. In this case, these detailed product specifications were completed only a few days prior to launching the product. No matter, I never tire of clarifying the goals of a project, and, as long as nothing's shipped yet, it's never too late to finalize the agreement about what is to be delivered.

The final stages of a project, just prior to launch, are hair-raising enough without avoidable fire fighting. If you don't set and manage expectations, your stakeholders will be frustrated, and your team could fall victim to massive feature creep and dozens of urgent last-minute requests for additions just when you should be popping the champagne to celebrate the end of the project. So manage expectations from the moment you start the project, and don't let up until everyone's smiling and celebrating.

11 Lessons Not Learned

Learn from experience. Make new and more exciting mistakes each time!

"Smart people learn from experience; wise people learn from the experience of others."
– Dr. Ichak Adizes

Have you ever noticed that the topics raised at project post mortems tend to be pretty much the same for every project? How many times can we "learn" that goals were unclear, that communication sucked, or that late changes to the requirements caused quality issues in the product? In fact, the same things happen so frequently that one web site actually offers a post-mortem survey. You can just give your team the survey and they can check off the idiotic things that happened... AGAIN. No need to analyze too deeply: all of the usual suspects are right there.

Schedules Slip. Frequently, the cause of today's project schedule slip can be found on the last project's "lessons learned" list. Time and again, project teams fall prey to the same unanticipated yet predictable delays. Like ants marching around the rim of a glass, the scenery begins to look awfully familiar. How many times does it take to "learn" that people take vacations in the summer, that less work gets done during the holidays, and that individuals tend to fall ill during the winter? How often must we run a project with only one design spin or one QA test cycle built into the schedule before we realize that the odds of needing two or more are practically 100%? Organizations have an amazing ability to combine a great many intelligent people into an aggregate that has the intelligence and memory of an insect. (No offense intended to the insects!)

Hope is Not a Strategy. My speculation is that the "lessons not learned" phenomenon is a result of perpetual hopefulness, mass amnesia, or an unabashed lack of humility about how much less talented the previous team was. Whatever the cause, allowing your team to fail for entirely predictable reasons is inexcusable.

Since it always seems to be the same "lessons," I've started doing lessons learned at the beginning of the project and then managing the project to ensure that these problems don't occur again. After all, who wants to make the same old boring mistakes over and over? I much prefer making new and more exciting mistakes.

If You Fail, Fail in New and Exciting Ways! Failing due to unpredictable surprises is disappointing, but failing due to predictable, avoidable, and recurring mistakes seriously undermines morale and productivity. Teams become understandably cynical when they give their heart and soul to a project only to see it led down a well-worn path of past project errors.

If on-time delivery is critical to success, the project leader must facilitate the creation of a challenging yet achievable schedule that enjoys the commitment of the people who must carry it out. It can be done, and it MUST be done! Here are five easy ways to ensure that your project schedule doesn't end up on the "I could have told you so" scrap heap:

1. Use Goldratt's Theory of Constraints, exploring potential risks and accelerators, to create schedules that explicitly incorporate risk and upside in an obvious and unmistakable way. Humans need help to make accurate estimates. Make allowances for known biases in human estimating capabilities, and enable your team to make better estimates by the way in which you ask for their inputs.

2. Avoid the Frankenstein Schedule. Don't give up the most powerful leverage that you have in scheduling: the opportunity to optimize the overall path to solution captured in the PERT chart before squeezing individual tasks. Include the cross-functional parties in a shared dialogue about the most advantageous overall schedule, rather than stitching together independently-prepared Gantt charts from each functional silo.

3. Be absolutely committed to achieving the business-driven schedule that the executives require, but make sure that it is based on a sound plan, not wishful thinking. Executives will push for the business goals to be met, but you must engage them in a dialogue about how to achieve these goals by design, not wishing and hoping. The honest, albeit awkward, discussions that ensue will increase the respect between them and the project team, and put an end to "The Lying Game."

4. Launch pre-emptive strikes against disaster. Start preventing and mitigating schedule slip at the very first moment that you become aware that the schedule may slip; that's usually the first day of the project.

5. Review the "Lessons Learned" from previous projects, and scrutinize the schedule to ensure that the same time bombs are not planted in the current project plan.

The Fearless Project Leader's Defining Moment. When a project is shaping up to be the next Titanic, it's time to have a frank dialogue about the nature of reality with those people who are asking, and sometimes demanding, the patently ridiculous. When it becomes clear that thought and reason are not driving demands and decision-making, get out your truth serum and prepare to tell it like it is.

Sometimes it is an uphill battle to get others to understand the realities of the project plan. In my opinion, a fearless project leader who has learned from their previous projects can win the battle almost every time. Here are the secrets of fearless project leadership that can persuade others to earnestly consider your perspective.

Planning is the most often skipped phase of projects. It's a proven fact that, given a choice, most people will under-plan or do no planning at all. Ensure that the team has left no stone unturned in the planning phase. This means explicitly including risk and uncertainty in the plan, especially in the budget and schedule, if those items are critical to the project success.

As project leader, you must insist that your team devote appropriate attention to planning, not just what can go wrong and all of the potential obstacles, but how to improve the chances of success. Too often we think of all the ways that things can go wrong, but fail to explore what can go right. While single-number estimates are always wrong, stochastic estimation techniques and a healthy dose of both negativity and possibility-thinking should cover the bases between worst case, most likely case, and the best case. This provides a defendable position for the inevitable (and appropriate!) executive pushback and subsequent negotiations.

"The engineers REALLY wanted to have some defined processes to guide us in developing new products. That surprised me. I expected them to be uninterested or even hostile. But they were passionate about putting some ground rules and definitions in place to reduce all the misunderstandings and wasted time. They were equally clear about keeping those ground rules lightweight and flexible. So we iterated until we reached something that product managers, software developers, engineering and operations all could live with. We didn't let it die or forget about it....instead, we've been using it and building on it for the past year and have really seen results."

Stephanie Oberg, Senior Technical Program Manager, Lab126

Depict the plan with simplicity and clarity, so it can be understood even by someone who has not spent hours poring over it. It should be obvious to an executive who spends 15 seconds looking at your plan what the few critical issues are. The best way I have found to accomplish this is to have a one-page simplified flow chart of the high-level project critical-chain (critical-path and nearest neighbors most likely to compete for critical-path) from start to finish. While Microsoft Project is a handy tool to those who are familiar with it, most executives won't take the time to understand the intricacies of the interdependencies illustrated by its Gantt charts and PERT charts. Although it's almost twice the work, I find a simple diagram showing the critical-path (like the one in Graphic 9) is easier to follow, and worth its weight in gold when having a dialogue with executives.

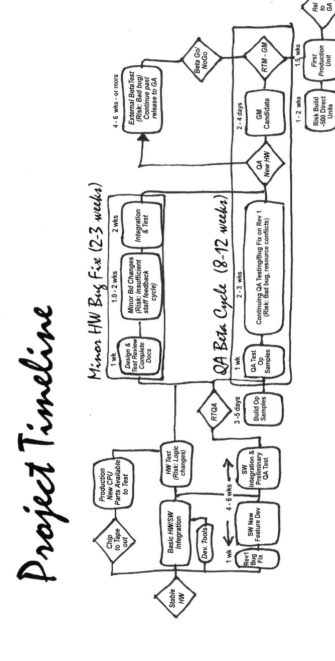

Graphic 9: Project Timeline with Duration Range Estimates

SCRAPPY TIP: *Ornament the biggest risk areas to the project with clip art such as a skull and crossbones, an ambulance, or a ticking time bomb. While you may be labeled a bit dramatic, these visuals will draw people's attention to the startling surprises that may await your project.*

And the final secret: never say no, even to the most ridiculous demands. Always say, "Yes, that's possible if..." and then explain the interdependencies and impacts. For example, if an executive insists that a project must be completed two months earlier than the high-confidence estimated completion date, I might say something like, "Sure, that's totally possible if you can tolerate a 90% chance of missing that date, or if you add an additional QA shift during the testing phase." They may balk at the requests, but at least you are now in a dialogue about how to jointly accomplish the project goals rather than an argument about whether or not it can be done. Remember, Gumperson's Law states that nothing is impossible to the person who doesn't have to do it. It can ALWAYS be done, albeit with differing levels of risk, failure, and heroics.

Review Your Reasons. Sometimes, as a result of executive pushback, it makes sense to go away and re-examine your plan to see if there are areas that you missed. However, if you have done #1 and #2 of the above correctly, you should be able to say with confidence, "I totally understand the business need for what you are asking, and I truly hope that we HAVE overlooked something in our planning that makes our conclusions about completion date (or budget, or whatever the issue is) erroneous and overly pessimistic. Help us out here. What did we miss? (Motion to your one-page plan, with the skulls, ambulances, and time bombs.) Help us understand where our assumptions are incorrect."

Sensible, reasonable executives interested in fact-based decisions will offer creative suggestions that may indeed point out where assumptions could be changed in order to better achieve the goals. Other, more bumbling types may show their true nature here with red-faced fist-pounding, intimidation, or abdication of responsibility that leaves the burden squarely on the project team. In the latter case, wage slaves are destined to go off and "do their best" until the project's inevitable demise. For these unlucky souls, from this point on it is not so much a matter of leading the project, but merely documenting the debacle. Experienced project managers come to realize that it's easier to slip the schedule later. At the beginning, everyone knows that the schedule is ridiculous, but no one is allowed to admit it, so they just wait until it's undeniable. But don't use this tactic. It's a sure way to lose the respect of your team and get your "Scrappy Project Management" membership card revoked.

Knowing is Not Doing. Just knowing what mistakes were made in the previous project is not enough. Knowledge alone changes nothing unless it is put into action. You'll never lose weight by reading a diet book.

There's always some reason why well-intentioned, educated, experienced professionals are doing the opposite of what they know makes sense. Frequently it's because they are really busy and can't possibly do what needs to be done until someone else changes first—usually their boss, or someone in a different department. "If only" someone or something else would change, then they would be able to do what they need to do to accomplish the goals. Certainly the fundamental attribution error is partially to blame, but what's the rest of the story?

Jeffrey Pfeffer and Robert Sutton wrote a whole book on *The Knowing-Doing Gap* when they realized that their colleagues at the Stanford Business School didn't follow the principles they taught when they themselves led companies. The same thing happens in project teams, too.

"Well done is better than well said." – Benjamin Franklin

The Knowing-Doing Gap. For a good chunk of the last 20 years of my life, I've managed to achieve outrageously successful results by doing nothing more extraordinary than applying what I've learned from people who are much smarter than me. Based on my years of experience, I've come up with a couple of ideas about why people don't put what they know into practice. With apologies to those physicists out there who will mumble, "a three-legged stool doesn't wobble" and other incomprehensible things about degrees of freedom in mechanical systems, I use a four-legged stool to explain these hindrances. You'll recognize some of these ideas from previous chapters. The four legs on the stool causing the knowing-doing gap, and preventing people from crossing it, are:

- **Learned Helplessness:** This is characterized by "It's not my fault!" and "They are doing it to me!" thinking. It's a conviction that, although you know how to do a job, certain conditions completely beyond your control do not permit you to do it.

- **Fear of Failure:** If you're not allowed to fail, you must be extremely vigilant about what you start, so you avoid starting something worthwhile, lest you should fail.

- **Aversion to Planning:** Studies have proven that, given a choice, people prefer not to plan. At the same time, we also know that planning dramatically improves results. But, hey, it's just no fun planning when you can be hyperactively aimless.

- **Instinct for Competition:** Win-lose thinking is the first instinct for many people in any negotiation. (I'm not talking about solving the Middle East peace crisis here. Any joint decision-making or problem-solving is a negotiation, and we all negotiate many times a day with our teammates.) Doing better than others occupies our time while making real progress takes a back seat. Fear of losing, coupled with a lack of clear goals, prevents people from even playing the game.

Lead Like the Pros. The difference between someone occupying a project leadership position and a professional project leader is that the professionals do what is required. No matter what. Whether they feel like it or not. Whether they think they have time or not. Whether it puts them at risk or not. With no excuses. How can project leaders enable people on their teams to cross that gap? Here are some ideas:

1. Challenge people to consider their own contribution to the circumstances that are keeping them stuck. We're all part of the problem.

2. Confront them with their own power to effect change to these circumstances. We're all part of the solution. (My undergraduate chemistry days are coming back to me as I write, and I just can't resist writing, "If you're not part of the solution, you're part of the precipitate!" Well, it was funny at the time.)

3. Distinguish fact from interpretation. Hold a rubber chicken at shoulder height and then let it go. Ask, "What caused it to fall?" Gravity is one possible explanation, and the victim's story. "I let go" is equally true, and a much more empowering perspective. We can focus on things that we can't control, like gravity, but that leaves us stuck in the role of a victim. Help your team understand that they are choosing their interpretation of their circumstances, and hopelessness and helplessness are just one possible way to look at a situation.

4. Exercise your ability to perceive a range of possible perspectives in any situation by developing both extremely negative and ridiculously positive interpretations of a particular circumstance. You will soon discover that reality is much more a choice of which story we choose to tell ourselves than a fact. When something "bad" happens, ask, "What does this make possible that wasn't possible before?" Sometimes you can't tell good luck from bad luck when it's happening.

5. Counteract the fear of failure with encouragement to avoid the sure loss that will come from doing nothing. Humans have a tendency to avoid a sure loss. Continually assert that the most dangerous thing to do is to stay in the comfort zone.

6. Determine if there is anything that you are more committed to than merely being comfortable, more than maintaining the status quo. (There usually is something!)

7. Overcome the natural aversion to planning by implementing a system of accountability with another person, or within the organization, that acknowledges planning as "real work." It is, but no code is written, no sheet metal cut, or no circuit designed while it is occurring, so it can be tempting to skip it. Find someone who will call you on the carpet if you get sloppy.

8. Raise awareness of the human tendency toward competition, even when the result is less than that which can be achieved through collaboration. A simple thumb-wrestling experiment should suffice. Ask pairs of people to thumb wrestle and offer $1000 for each time they pin their opponent's thumbs down during a 15-second contest. Most will struggle against one another, but a few will realize that if they cooperate their winnings will far exceed those of the victor in the pairs playing a win-lose game. Help your people understand that collaboration is almost never the first instinct, and almost always yields a higher-quality result.

It doesn't matter how much your team knows if they can't execute. Over 70% of business failures have been attributed to an inability to execute.[13] If knowing how to do something were enough, we'd all be rich and thin. We must be able to implement what we know, whether we feel like it or not, whether we think there's time to do what needs to be done or not. Action and results beat a great theory any day.

Alas, as I've said before, common sense is not common practice. If you want to achieve outrageous and amazing results time and time again, you need a recipe for success. If you've learned your lessons right, you'll do it right the second time around. That way you'll be ahead of the newbies on the block, and those condemned to eternal damnation who won't learn from their mistakes.

---

13. Charan, R., & Colvin, G., "Why CEOs Fail," *Fortune*, 139(12), June 21, 1999, p. 68-78.

12 Sure We Appreciate You – Didn't You Get Your Paycheck?

Attitude of Gratitude: Celebrate project success... and some failures, too!

> *"The important thing to remember is that if you don't have that inspired enthusiasm that is contagious, whatever you do have is also contagious." – Danny Cox*

When we're enjoying summer in the northern hemisphere, my mind naturally wanders to picnics, parties, and celebrations of every kind. I don't need a very big reason to throw a party. It's genetic—finding six matching wine glasses in my kitchen cabinet is reason enough.

Projects are fertile territory for all manner of festivities. For example, if you live long enough, you'll eventually complete a project successfully. When the customer is delighted beyond words, when the i's have been dotted, the t's crossed, and the seemingly endless task list is dwindling to mere trifles, it's time to celebrate. What's the best way for you and your team to mark such an accomplishment? How should the tireless souls who made it possible be recognized and appreciated? I have a few ideas.

Congratulations! On to the Next Impossible Project. Don't ruin the fleeting bliss of a successful project completion by "celebrating" it all wrong. Before I start with the Do's of celebration, let me clearly spell out the Don'ts.

While there are many ways to celebrate project success, the one I am least fond of is assigning the team to the next demanding project. The reward for doing a great job shouldn't be to get stuck with the next gnarly task. After the death march, at least hold a wake. Take some time, spend a few bucks, have a little shindig. The next project can wait another 24 hours!

My second least favorite way of commemorating the completion of some back-breaking project from hell is to receive yet another T-shirt with the project name and some geeky logo on it. I've accumulated dozens of them over the years. OK, I realize that there are those of you out there whose entire wardrobe consists of such garments, but personally I've never found much use for them aside from washing my car. How about a nice strappy sundress, thong, or halter top for everyone on the team? Perhaps an upscale collection of the latest shades of eye make-up? I'm sure you get my point.

While we're on the subject, please be assured that I don't need another little metal flashlight, fancy pen, key chain, pocket knife, or any kind of coffee mug with the company logo on it—with apologies to those of you whose kitchens are fully outfitted with such mugs. Garage sales are teeming with these lovingly-selected trinkets. And I never did need cuff links, a man's watch, or a block of Lucite (no matter what's suspended in it). How many landfills will it take to dispose of all of this? Enough is enough. It's time to be a little more creative in expressing our gratitude. At least make sure that the doo-dads that you're giving out are edible, drinkable, recyclable, or at the very least, biodegradable.

Show Me the Money? Let's mull over the purpose of recognition, appreciation, and celebration in a project. I personally think it's to thank and appreciate the team for their work, to reinforce their initiative and results, and to inspire them to continue delivering similar results in the future. Ultimately it's about motivation, so we had better know something about what motivates people. Contrary to popular belief, and fortunately for those of us on tight budgets, it's not cash.

Bob Nelson, author of *1001 Ways to Reward Employees*, reports that cash is lower on the list of motivating rewards than sincere notes of thanks. But quite a few people are still under the impression that it's all about money. "Thank me in my paycheck!" is their mercenary cry. Unfortunately, it's been proven time and again that stashing a little extra cash in someone's paycheck isn't very effective. Money is too much like a regular salary for doing the job to be seen as a sign of sincere gratitude. It's like oxygen, never greatly appreciated until it's gone. Cash is by nature a solitary reward that's more wisely enjoyed in secrecy, lest someone who received less—or none at all—feel jilted. And monetary rewards are quickly forgotten, especially when rolled into a person's regular paycheck.

If you must use cash as a reward, perhaps due to a seasonal scarcity of T-shirts or coffee mugs in your local area, there are a few guidelines to follow in order to be more effective. First, make sure to award it separately from the regular paycheck so it doesn't look like some kind of accounting error or a change in tax status. Then find the highest-ranking person around who knows something about the project, and ask them to hand over the money while jabbering on with a few specific words of appreciation about the contribution that inspired this reward.

Finally, make sure that the amount is inconsequential compared with the person's monthly paycheck—enough for them to say "Wow, thanks!" but not so much that it causes a heart attack. There are two reasons for this.

First, it's important that the cash is clearly a token of your appreciation, not some kind of substitute for fair compensation. People who have been slaving away for months, whose health has suffered, whose spouse is about to divorce them for never being home, whose kids barely recognize them, will not be amused to think that you have put a price on their misery.

Second, when other people find out about the amount of the reward, they won't be as irritated that you didn't give them any, or quite as much. It's a mathematical impossibility, but in my experience nearly everyone thinks they are above average. You're bound to overlook someone, and even the undeserving frequently assume that they have something coming to them.

Better Than Cold, Hard Cash. If you want to recognize individuals, gift certificates for a nice restaurant or a day at the spa make a greater impact than money. They usually come in a fancy envelope, can be savored by the recipient for weeks or months before cashing them in, and ultimately result in a memorable couple of hours of enjoyment.

But team rewards are by far the easiest and least complicated option. While it might be appropriate to take a few particularly deserving individuals aside to express heartfelt appreciation for their special efforts, creating celebrations that focus on the team will be perceived as a lot more fair, and will cause significantly fewer headaches. Even giving away T-shirts, which I have already disparaged, is not without pitfalls. On one project, I had 12 people on the core team, and about 40 on the extended team, but when it came time to give out T-shirts there were at least 120 people who expected one.

There won't be any hurt feelings when the core team, extended team, and dozens of "voyeurs" are invited on a dinner cruise, or spend an afternoon golfing, or throw all caution to the wind and go bowling together. People can bring their significant others (if they're still speaking), hang out, have some fun, and repair slightly tattered relationships. The frustrations that people may have felt with each other during the project can melt into minor irritations under the influence of a little beer and the flicker of the fluorescent lights of the bowling alley. During the celebration, it may dawn on folks that no amount of cruising, golfing, or bowling could possibly make up for the humongous amount of work they just completed, but they'll usually appreciate your thoughtfulness in arranging the event nonetheless. You might want to arrange for a team photo, a certificate with an inspirational saying on it, or a personal note from the CEO to be presented to each person attending. Just make sure that you have someone PhotoShop in those people who were out of town when you took the picture. (Easy to do in today's digital age.)

Better Yet — Peer-to-Peer Appreciation. The humdingers of reward and appreciation methods are those where team members reward each other. These peer-to-peer recognition systems enable individuals to express their gratitude to each other when they catch someone in the act of doing something that supports the goals of the team. This reduces perceived favoritism by managers and increases personal responsibility for assuring that an attitude of gratitude prevails among team members. Here's how to make it easy.

1. Print out a stack of certificates that say something like "Thanks a Bazillion! You made a difference to me!" Leave a bunch where people can pick one up, fill in the particulars of the person's name and what they did that was praiseworthy, then award it with a flourish. People really appreciate the sincere thanks of a colleague for a job well done, and don't part willingly with this evidence that they are truly valued. I've seen wrinkled and yellowing versions of these adorning cubicles years after they were received.

2. Get a pile of Starbucks® gift certificates and have an admin person keep them handy. Let people know that anyone can pick one up and award it to anyone else for any reason just by signing them out with the admin. All they need to do is verbally thank the person and hand over the booty. A monthly review of the tracking sheet is plenty to discourage gaming the system, and it's amazingly easy to administer. At $5 or $10 a pop, the total budget for this usually ends up being less than the cost of post-notes in the supply cabinet.

3. Combine both of the above for even more impact.

Celebrating in the Global Village. Don't forget team members on the other side of the ocean when celebrating. It's easy to overlook remote team members, but they are an increasingly important part of project success. With a little imagination, a transcontinental expression of gratitude can be arranged. Send handwritten notes of thanks. Ship sweets from your local area. YouTube a video of a "team song" acknowledging their work with creative words set to a classic Rolling Stones tune. Dress the part for added impact.

Or arrange a little party for them. In every country of the world there are people who enjoy planning a party. Find that person, give them a budget, and set them loose planning something that the local folks will enjoy and appreciate. Post pictures of your parties on the company intranet and include the pictures as the lead-in to the post-project-review where a few smiling faces will be a welcome counterpoint to some of the dreary memories that will be dredged up by the retrospective.

Never Reward Firefighters! Adrenaline junkies in search of their next fix, these people will actually cause problems just to have the thrill of fixing them and being rewarded for it. Not consciously, mind you. Although, I have heard of one engineer renowned for designing something that didn't work quite right, and then submitting a quality improvement suggestion on how to fix his own designs. Amazingly, the quality manager rewarded him for this! How embarrassing is that? And how demotivating to others. Firefighters carry matches. Don't encourage them!

Reward is a double-edged sword: what gets rewarded is what gets done. If the number of calls answered per hour is the metric used to reward customer support folks, guess what happens? They give customers the bum's rush off the phone, or even hang up on them. Reward the number of bugs fixed? How about focusing on preventing bugs! Don't reward anything that you don't want more of in your project.

Firefighting, diving catches, and heroics are symptoms of a problem, not signs of a cure. Don't spread this disease by rewarding the carriers. Find the person who is planning ahead, preventing disaster, executing with excellence, and recovering from setbacks without setting their hair on fire, without glitz or fanfare. Whip out a Starbucks® gift certificate for this everyday hero and send them home at 3 PM to enjoy some time with their kids.

Celebrate Early and Often. Not unlike the person who eats dessert first, I believe in celebrating the success of a project early in its lifecycle. If celebration, recognition, and appreciation are truly going to be motivating, it just won't do to save it all up until the end. People need about ten times more experiences of positive feedback for every one piece of negative feedback for the amounts to feel equal. It's far more effective to sprinkle a little appreciation fairy dust along the way.

Practice an attitude of gratitude. Notice what's going well, and keep the psychological scales balanced by offering some encouraging words to those responsible. A handwritten note every week or two, expressing sincere thanks for some helpful deed, won't break the recognition and appreciation bank. And a monthly Team Decompression Session at a local park or grubby pub would be well worth the money, even if it has to come out of your own pocket.

Innovative Appreciation Techniques. The most highly-appreciated reward that I've ever seen used was on-site chair massages for almost a hundred strung-out people, during an extremely harrowing project phase. Everyone was deeply touched by this gesture, including big tough guys whom we worried might not appreciate it. Even the stodgiest of the team enjoyed their experience and were blown away that a company would do something so extraordinary for their people.

Another energizing celebration is a facilitated drum circle with a bunch of big-ass drums and a space where people can make a whole lot of noise without the police showing up. Hire a professional to cart in the drums and lead the tribe in making sufficient racket to wake the dead. It's a great stress-reliever too, and even if people don't like the drumming they'll still enjoy watching everyone else make total fools of themselves. Bring some earplugs for the noise-averse-there are always a few.

Try something a little whimsical to keep spirits up in otherwise tiresome projects. Sometimes amusement is its own reward. On one project called "Columbo," we held a "Being Columbo" costume contest. While we expected to have quite a few people sporting trench coats in honor of the TV show detective popular at that time, we were amazed when one creative engineer showed up dressed as a giant loaf of "Columbo" bread, inspired by a local bakery of that name. Another team created a "comedy corridor" where people were required to sport clown noses, tell jokes, and otherwise engage in uproarious behavior.

Of course, playing laser tag is a heart-pounding thrill. Laser tag is the great equalizer. People of wildly diverse cultures seem to enjoy running around in the dark, shooting each other with lasers. No matter how serene and sedate a team member appears to be, once they are cloaked in the darkness of a laser tag arena it's open season on anything that moves.

When all else fails, have everyone get together to eat pizza. Pizza is comfort food. Everyone feels better after a slice or two.

Making a Real Difference is the Best Reward. On one of my many travels to Japan, I was fortunate enough to work with an R&D team in a company that makes bathroom fixtures. Being a high-tech kind of gal, I mused about how people could get enthusiastic about making fancy toilets. As I walked into their main lobby I encountered a 4-foot wide glass ball containing a toilet, one of their featured products. Nearby there was a giant papier-mâché toilet lit from within, built for a festival. A little farther down the hall was the ultimate display: a toilet that opened automatically via a motion sensor when someone walked by. The sign out front even spelled out the company name in little ceramic toilets. Wow! It was pretty clear that these people were passionate about their products. At first I thought this was mildly amusing, but as I worked with them I realized that they were not just making toilets, they were (and are!) revolutionizing the concept of the bathroom experience for their customers. They have a bold new vision of what a bathroom can be, and how it can make a positive difference in the lives of their customers. Who knew?!

As project leaders, this is exactly the kind of passion, enthusiasm, and commitment that we need to inspire in the people in our teams. If people can be sincerely committed to transforming the world through toilets, I'm sure you can find a way to evoke the passionate commitment of your team to whatever project you lead. Try asking a provocative question of your team, like, "Who cares whether we do this project or not?" or, "Why bother to do it?" If you can't find reasons beyond, "Because we're getting paid to do it," then you're missing one of the greatest sources of motivation: the perception that people are making a meaningful difference. You can be a janitor sweeping the floors at NASA, or you can be helping to put a man on the moon. You can be a bricklayer or on a team building a cathedral. You can be developing a profitable new drug, or saving lives. It's all a matter of interpretation. Make your team feel like heroes.

Most individuals and teams in the professional world are deeply committed to doing a good job because they have pride in their work. Too much focus on external rewards can reduce the intrinsic motivation of individuals. Pay your kids $5 to mow the lawn once, and they'll never do it for free again. Don't turn your people into reward-and-recognition junkies by supplying them with too many tangible rewards, or by being insincere with your praise. Remember, the most powerful motivational tools at a project manager's disposal are free. According to Bob Nelson's research, more money and job security aren't at the tippity top of the list of the kind of recognition employees most desire. They most covet your personal support, being involved in what's going on, a sincere word of appreciation for a job well done, maybe a pizza party from time to time. They long to be allowed to decide what they need to do and how to do it. They sparkle when you express some genuine concern for them by providing flexible working hours, time off on the weekends, an occasional note of praise, a public word of appreciation, or simply making time for them to answer their questions or just get to know them as human beings.[14]

---

14. Nelson, Bob, *1001 Ways to Reward Employees*, (New York: Workman Publishing, 1994), p. 2. See http://www.nelson-motivation.com/ for more.

Celebrate Failure, too! With innovation being so important to today's projects, I wonder why we don't see more people celebrating failures. Innovation is a risky process, and guaranteed to fail from time to time-so why only reward success? Failure is frequently the foundation upon which future successes are built. Truly innovative teams learn to "fail forward," lurching fitfully in the direction of their goals. If we only celebrate successes, we may inadvertently discourage experimenting and taking appropriate risks. No amount of exhortation about the importance of risk-taking will communicate a stronger message than one clear celebration of a dismal failure from which critical information was learned. Don't celebrate the same stupid mistakes made over and over again, those lessons not learned that get repeated on every project. Celebrate new and more exciting mistakes that lay the groundwork for the next breakthrough!

As long as people's basic compensation needs are being fairly met, skillfully applying a healthy and sincere attitude of gratitude will deliver more results than another raise, promotion, or bonus. Don't fall for the big lie that people want to be thanked in their paycheck. Ultimately, people want to be sincerely appreciated for their work, which they hope will make some positive difference in this world. Not only do our team members enjoy working on our projects more, but we ourselves are transformed when we turn more of our attention to what deserves our appreciation.

13 Wrap Up

Go Ahead, Get Scrappy!

"If opportunity came disguised as temptation, one knock would be enough." – Lane Olinghouse

I know a pilot who has flown 7,000 hours. The other day I asked him, "Chuck, the next time you fly are you going to use your pre-flight checklist?" "You bet!" he replied. Now why would a jet pilot with that much experience use a checklist? Because that's what professionals do. Professionals know that in the heat of battle much of our blood rushes to our arms and legs, where it is useful for hitting, kicking, and running (the fight or flight response), leaving little to nourish the one major advantage that we have over monkeys—our frontal lobes. Professionals do what needs to be done, regardless of whether they have time to do it (there's never enough), and regardless of whether they think other people will like it. One sure-fire way to get a busy team member to roll their eyes is to ask them if they have time to set clear goals, make a schedule, and discuss roles and responsibilities. People rarely think that they have time to pause and plan. Don't ask. Insist! Don't take a vote about whether your team should meet regularly to assure that everyone is on the same page. Schedule the meetings! It's the project leader's job to assure the team avoids predictable failure. A checklist, or a set of operating guidelines, is one way to instill this kind of discipline. It's a rock in a sea of flotsam and jetsam. It's the next best thing to being lucky.

Project management is a discipline that must be learned and practiced. It's the closest thing to running your own business, only with a lot less authority and a smaller paycheck. Many people think managing a project is just common sense. Most people think they have a good understanding of project management, even if they are not trained or experienced in it. They have opinions about how projects should be run, and freely offer those opinions unsolicited and with great vigor. Often wrong, but never in doubt, they think that their opinion is somehow on par with a blizzard of best-practices and decades of experience. Certain that "this company is different," they insist that standard wisdom doesn't apply to them. While they'd no more stand for you micro-managing their part of the project than they'd agree to a diet consisting solely of Metamucil®, they don't view their resistance to basic project management best practices as micro-managing your role. Oh, lucky you!

Optimize, Don't Maximize. When there is a critical mass of project management expertise in your work environment you can band together to support each other in doing what makes sense. In moments of self-doubt, your colleagues can reassure you that you are using sound judgment in your project leadership. When you are described as bureaucratic or "The Process Queen," your peers can remind you that the top reasons of project failure are entirely preventable and occur precisely because people lack the discipline to do what is required. They can reinforce your conviction that the right amount of process delivers far better results than just doing your best. Aim for just enough process to optimize the results, not a drop more, but not a drop less either. Don't do something just because it is a project management best practice. Do it because it is the right thing for the project at the time. Generate only documents that will be used for some purpose. Hold only effectively-run meetings with clear goals. Then, when you encounter resistance from those who detest process in any form, you will be able to say with a clear conscience that you are using the minimum sensible processes to get the job done.

Be the Voice of Reason. In small companies, often the greatest challenge of project leadership results when there is only one person in the company who really understands what it takes to provide effective project management. There are frequently numerous inexperienced people vigorously inserting their uninformed opinions about what is required and what is excessive process. As the lone voice of project management, you may find yourself defending the basics to these PM backseat drivers on issues like setting priorities, having clear metrics of success, or the need to hold design reviews or track action items. Hunch-based decision-making and the tyranny of the urgent reign supreme in these environments, and woe be unto the courageous project leader who throws himself in front of the careening caravan of confident but misguided second-guessers. This is exactly the time to clutch your Scrappy Project Management Checklist to your heart and stagger toward the finish line with dogged determination. Passion, commitment, and discipline separate the highly-paid-secretary type of project manager from the true heart-and-soul project leader.

Although we've been calling it "project management," I've always liked the folk wisdom, "You manage cows. You lead people." Project leaders know that their people deserve practical and responsible projects because it dramatically increases their chances of success. Project leaders take responsibility for more than schedule, scope, and budget. They are committed to their people, regardless of reporting relationship. Fearless project leaders stand their ground and insist on a fact-based project plan. They have the quiet confidence to assert that the business results must rest on a sound estimate, not on wishing and hoping. This is the only responsible way to conduct business in a project, and it is an absolute must for anyone wishing to emerge with his or her integrity intact.

When All Else Fails. Sometimes the responsible thing is to take your skills elsewhere. In one such experience, I presented clear plans, schedules, assumptions, risks and possible accelerators, along with my conclusions, to the CEO-only to have him retort, "I don't buy it." That was it. He offered no reasons or information about how his assumptions and beliefs differed from mine. Not long thereafter, I moved on. Never try to teach a pig to sing. It wastes your time and annoys the pig.

Sometimes reason doesn't prevail. My advice? When the horse is dead—get off! Some projects aren't worthy of your fearless leadership. Move on to your next great opportunity. You can't enlighten the unconscious! But if you decide to throw yourself heart and soul into some worthy cause, remember, you can turn a project from crappy to scrappy just by adding an "s."

SCRAPPY TIP: *If you are going to be a great project manager, you'd better keep your backbone intact. Be prepared to be respected but not necessarily liked, and keep your resume up to date!*

The Scrappy Project Management Checklist. There are many people passing themselves off as project leaders who are merely occupying the position without being willing to take a stand and do the right thing in the face of opposition and temptations. If you want to be the kind of project leader who inspires commitment from your team, hope from your stakeholders, and the admiration of your colleagues, these common-sense guidelines for project management excellence will serve you well:

- Be completely & unrepentantly obsessed with the "customer."

- Provide shared, measurable, challenging & achievable goals as clear as sunlight.

- Engage in effective, vociferous & unrelenting communication with all stakeholders.

- Ensure that roles & responsibilities are unmistakably understood and agreed upon by all.

- Create viable plans & schedules that enjoy the team's hearty commitment.

- Mitigate big, hairy, abominable risks & implement innovative accelerators.

- Prioritize ruthlessly, choosing between heart, lungs & kidneys if necessary.

- Anticipate and accommodate necessary and inevitable change.

- Challenge assumptions & beliefs, especially insidious self-imposed limitations.

- Manage the expectations of all stakeholders: under-promise & over-deliver.

- Learn from experience. Make new and more exciting mistakes each time!

- Attitude of Gratitude: Celebrate project success... and some failures, too!

SCRAPPY TIP: *To dramatically improve your odds of achieving success—even during the most challenging projects—sleep with The Scrappy Project Management Checklist under your pillow. Dream of the success you are poised to achieve while embracing the checklist concepts; wake up, and make the dream come true!*

Parting Thought. Leading a project successfully without this kind of toolkit is like trying to design an integrated circuit with pencil and paper. A fool with a tool is still a fool, but perhaps we won't make such foolish mistakes with a guide during the wild and woolly experience of leading a challenging project. What does it take beyond a checklist?

DISCIPLINE: This toolkit, and the discipline to apply it consistently and depart from it thoughtfully, will make you and your teams a lot more "lucky," as much as doubling your chances of success.

COMMITMENT: Your commitment to doing what is required time and again, whether you feel like it or not, whether people totally support you in this or not, will distinguish you as a true project management professional.

PASSION: The enthusiasm of the project leader is contagious. Projects are hard work! Your team deserves a leader who is completely and authentically passionate about the project.

Passionate, disciplined, and totally committed—now that truly describes the Scrappy Project Manager. The road is sometimes rocky and treacherous. Everyone gets discouraged from time to time. When you feel like giving up, hang in there for at least five minutes longer. And if you do fail, remember what Winston Churchill said: *"Success consists of going from failure to failure with no loss of enthusiasm."*

Ride it like you stole it, baby! - *Kimberly*

 SCRAPPY ABOUT

Index

About the Author

Kimberly Wiefling is the founder of Wiefling Consulting, LLC, a scrappy global consulting enterprise committed to enabling her clients to achieve highly unlikely or darn near impossible results predictably and repeatedly. Her company has helped individuals, teams, and organizations realize their dreams through a combination of courageous leadership, project management excellence, sheer determination, and plain old stubbornness. She has worked with companies of all sizes, including one-person ventures and those in the Fortune 50, and she has helped to launch and grow more than half a dozen startups, a few of which are reaping excellent profits at this very moment.

Kimberly attributes her scrappiness to being raised in Pittsburgh, Pennsylvania and to the sheer luck of genetics—her whole family is seriously scrappy. (Thanks, Mom and Dad!) A physicist by education, she earned a Master's degree in Physics from Case Institute and a Bachelor's in Chemistry and Physics from Wright State University. Kimberly spent a decade at HP in engineering leadership, product development, and project management roles. She then spent four years in the wild and crazy world of Silicon Valley start-ups before leading one to a glorious defeat during the dotcom bust of 2001 as the VP of Program Management. (Indeed, the company was purchased by Google, but as luck would have it, for pennies on the dollar... Drat!) Vigorously scrappy, she reemerged from the smoldering remains of the "Silicon Valley Mood Disorder" to launch her own company, consulting worldwide from Tokyo to Armenia, as well as the once-again-vibrant Silicon Valley.

Kimberly is the executive editor of The Scrappy Guides™, and a regular contributor to Project-Connections.com. She is also the lead blogger on the UC Santa Cruz Extension's The Art of Project Management Blog.[15] Feel free to contact her in person at kimberly@wiefling.com.

---

15. www.SVProjectManagement.net

Create Thought Leadership for Your Company

Books deliver instant credibility to the author. Having an MBA or PhD is great, however, putting the word "author" in front of your name is similar to using the letters PhD or MBA. You are no long Michael Green, you are "Author Michael Green."

Books give you a platform to stand on. They help you to:

- Demonstrate your thought leadership
- Generate leads

Books deliver increased revenue, particularly indirect revenue

- A typical consultant will make 3x in indirect revenue for every dollar they make on book sales

Books are better than a business card. They are:

- More powerful than white papers
- An item that makes it to the book shelf vs. the circular file
- The best tchotchke you can give at a conference

Why wait to write your book?

Check out other companies that have built credibility by writing and publishing a book through Happy About:

Contact Happy About at 408-257-3000 or go to http://happyabout.info.

Other Happy About Books

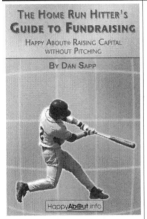

Learn How to Present Yourself to Get Funding!

This is a step-by-step guide to help you have the conversation you need to secure the capital you want.

Paperback $19.95
eBook $11.95

Produce Innovation at Your Company!

This book helps you to identify, manage and overcome the debilitating inventoritis condition and explains how to become an effective product marketer in the process.

Paperback:$19.95
eBook: $11.95

Postscript

Congratulations on making it all the way to the end of this book!

Now you know how to be scrappy, but here's the real test—putting what you know into action! I know as well as anyone that it takes real courage to implement these practices, and there will be days when you may not feel like you have a scrappy bone in your body. No worries! Live out of your commitments, not your courage. Every day make a renewed commitment to what you believe in, what you stand for, what other people can count on you for, and then go about living up to those high expectations—or falling short of them, and getting back up and stumbling forward when necessary. Reach, stretch, learn and grow every single day. Beware of the creeping temptation to settle for anything less than your scrappy best. Shine like the blazing sun that you are!

And if you'd like to write your own Scrappy About book, please contact me:

kimberly@wiefling.com

Stay Scrappy! — Kimberly

Made in the USA
Columbia, SC
13 May 2019